£10.95

NEW ACCENTS

General Editor: TERENCE HAWKES

Metafiction
The Theory and Practice
of Self-Conscious Fiction

IN THE SAME SERIES

Linguistics and the Novel   *Roger Fowler*
Language and Style   *E. L. Epstein*
Subculture: The Meaning of Style   *Dick Hebdige*
Science Fiction: Its Criticism and Teaching   *Patrick Parrinder*
The Semiotics of Theatre and Drama   *Keir Elam*
Translation Studies   *Susan Bassnett-McGuire*
Fantasy: The Literature of Subversion   *Rosemary Jackson*
Structuralism and Semiotics   *Terence Hawkes*
Critical Practice   *Catherine Belsey*
Formalism and Marxism   *Tony Bennett*
Reading Television   *John Fiske and John Hartley*
Sexual Fiction   *Maurice Charney*
Re-Reading English   *Edited by Peter Widdowson*
Deconstruction: Theory and Practice   *Christopher Norris*
Orality and Literacy   *Walter J. Ong*
Poetry as Discourse   *Antony Easthope*
Literature and Propaganda   *A. P. Foulkes*
Narrative Fiction: Contemporary Poetics
    Shlomith Rimmon-Kenan
Reception Theory: A Critical Introduction
    Robert C. Holub

Metafiction
The Theory and Practice
of Self-Conscious Fiction

PATRICIA WAUGH

METHUEN
London and New York

First published in 1984 by
Methuen & Co. Ltd
11 New Fetter Lane, London EC4P 4EE
Published in the USA by
Methuen & Co.
in association with Methuen, Inc.
733 Third Avenue, New York, NY 10017

Photoset by Rowland Phototypesetting Ltd
Bury St Edmunds, Suffolk
Printed in Great Britain by
Richard Clay (The Chaucer Press) Ltd
Bungay, Suffolk

British Library Cataloguing in Publication Data

Waugh, Patricia
    Metafiction.—(New accents)
    1. Fiction—Technique   2. Rhetoric
    I. Title   II. Series
    808.3   PN3355

    ISBN 0-416-32630-7
    ISBN 0-416-32640-4 Pbk

Library of Congress Cataloging in Publication Data

Waugh, Patricia.
    Metafiction : the theory and practice of
    self-conscious fiction.

    (New accents)
    Bibliography: p.
    Includes index
    1. Fiction.   I. Title.   II. Series: New accents
    (Methuen & Co.)
    PN3335.W38 1984   801'.953   84-9078

    ISBN 0-416-32630-7
    ISBN 0-416-32640-4 (Pbk.)

Contents

General editor's preface

It is easy to see that we are living in a time of rapid and radical social change. It is much less easy to grasp the fact that such change will inevitably affect the nature of those disciplines that both reflect our society and help to shape it.

Yet this is nowhere more apparent than in the central field of what may, in general terms, be called literary studies. Here, among large numbers of students at all levels of education, the erosion of the assumptions and presuppositions that support the literary disciplines in their conventional form has proved fundamental. Modes and categories inherited from the past no longer seem to fit the reality experienced by a new generation.

New Accents is intended as a positive response to the initiative offered by such a situation. Each volume in the series will seek to encourage rather than resist the process of change; to stretch rather than reinforce the boundaries that currently define literature and its academic study.

Some important areas of interest immediately present themselves. In various parts of the world, new methods of analysis have been developed whose conclusions reveal the limitations of the Anglo-American outlook we inherit. New concepts of literary forms and modes have been proposed; new notions of the nature of literature itself and of how it communicates are current; new views of literature's role in relation to society flourish. *New Accents* will aim to expound and comment upon the most notable of these.

In the broad field of the study of human communication, more and more emphasis has been placed upon the nature and function of the new electronic media. *New Accents* will try to identify and discuss the challenge these offer to our traditional modes of critical response.

The same interest in communication suggests that the series should also concern itself with those wider anthropological and sociological areas of investigation which have begun to involve scrutiny of the nature of art itself and of its relation to our whole way of life. And this will ultimately require attention to be focused on some of those activities which in our society have hitherto been excluded from the prestigious realms of Culture. The disturbing realignment of values involved and the disconcerting nature of the pressures that work to bring it about both constitute areas that *New Accents* will seek to explore.

Finally, as its title suggests, one aspect of *New Accents* will be firmly located in contemporary approaches to language, and a continuing concern of the series will be to examine the extent to which relevant branches of linguistic studies can illuminate specific literary areas. The volumes with this particular interest will nevertheless presume no prior technical knowledge on the part of their readers, and will aim to rehearse the linguistics appropriate to the matter in hand, rather than to embark on general theoretical matters.

Each volume in the series will attempt an objective exposition of significant developments in its field up to the present as well as an account of its author's own views of the matter. Each will culminate in an informative bibliography as a guide to further study. And, while each will be primarily concerned with matters relevant to its own specific interests, we can hope that a kind of conversation will be heard to develop between them; one whose accents may perhaps suggest the distinctive discourse of the future.

TERENCE HAWKES

Acknowledgements

I should like to acknowledge the help I have received from my colleagues Andrew Crisell and Derek Longhurst who have both commented usefully on the manuscript. I am particularly grateful to David Lodge who first inspired, and subsequently helped to sustain, my interest in metafiction, and to Terence Hawkes for his very painstaking and extremely helpful editorial guidance. Finally, I would like to dedicate this book to my husband Alec, who had never heard of metafiction when I met him but who now has a thorough appreciation of its significance in his life!

What is metafiction and why are they saying such awful things about it?

What is metafiction?

The thing is this.
That of all the several ways of beginning a book which are now in practice throughout the known world, I am confident my own way of doing it is the best – I'm sure it is the most religious – for I begin with writing the first sentence – and trusting to Almighty God for the second.

(Laurence Sterne, *Tristram Shandy*, p. 438)

Fuck all this lying look what I'm really trying to write about is writing not all this stuff . . .

(B. S. Johnson, *Albert Angelo*, p. 163)

Since I've started thinking about this story, I've gotten boils, piles, eye strain, stomach spasms, anxiety attacks. Finally I am consumed by the thought that at a certain point we all become nothing more than dying animals.

(Ronald Sukenick, *The Death of the Novel and Other Stories*, p. 49)

I remember once we were out on the ranch shooting peccadillos (result of a meeting, on the plains of the West, of the collared peccary and the nine-banded armadillo).

(Donald Barthelme, *City Life*, p. 4)

Fiction is woven into all ... I find this new reality (or unreality) more valid.

(John Fowles, *The French Lieutenant's Woman*, pp. 86–7)

If asked to point out the similarities amongst this disconcerting selection of quotations, most readers would immediately list two or three of the following: a celebration of the power of the creative imagination together with an uncertainty about the validity of its representations; an extreme self-consciousness about language, literary form and the act of writing fictions; a pervasive insecurity about the relationship of fiction to reality; a parodic, playful, excessive or deceptively naïve style of writing.

In compiling such a list, the reader would, in effect, be offering a brief description of the basic concerns and characteristics of the fiction which will be explored in this book. *Metafiction* is a term given to fictional writing which self-consciously and systematically draws attention to its status as an artefact in order to pose questions about the relationship between fiction and reality. In providing a critique of their own methods of construction, such writings not only examine the fundamental structures of narrative fiction, they also explore the possible fictionality of the world outside the literary fictional text.

Most of the quotations are fairly contemporary. This is deliberate. Over the last twenty years, novelists have tended to become much more aware of the theoretical issues involved in constructing fictions. In consequence, their novels have tended to embody dimensions of self-reflexivity and formal uncertainty. What connects not only these quotations but also all of the very different writers whom one could refer to as broadly 'metafictional', is that they all explore a *theory* of fiction through the *practice* of writing fiction.

The term 'metafiction' itself seems to have originated in an essay by the American critic and self-conscious novelist William H. Gass (in Gass 1970). However, terms like 'metapolitics', 'metarhetoric' and 'metatheatre' are a reminder of what has been, since the 1960s, a more general cultural interest in the problem of how human beings reflect, construct and mediate their experience of the world. Metafiction pursues such questions through its formal self-exploration, drawing on the traditional metaphor of the world as book, but often recasting it in the terms of contemporary philosophical, linguistic or literary theory. If, as individuals, we now occupy 'roles' rather than 'selves', then the study of characters in novels may provide a useful model for understanding the construction of subjectivity in the world outside novels. If our knowledge of this world is now seen to be mediated through language, then literary fiction (worlds constructed entirely of language) becomes a useful model for learning about the construction of 'reality' itself.

The present increased awareness of 'meta' levels of discourse and experience is partly a consequence of an increased social and cultural self-consciousness. Beyond this, however, it also reflects a greater awareness within contemporary culture of the function of language in constructing and maintaining our sense of everyday 'reality'. The simple notion that language passively reflects a coherent, meaningful and 'objective' world is no longer tenable. Language is an independent, self-contained system which generates its own 'meanings'. Its relationship to the phenomenal world is highly complex, problematic and regulated by convention. 'Meta' terms, therefore, are required in order to explore the relationship between this arbitrary linguistic system and the world to which it apparently refers. In fiction they are required in order to explore the relationship between the world *of* the fiction and the world *outside* the fiction.

In a sense, metafiction rests on a version of the Heisenbergian uncertainty principle: an awareness that 'for the smallest building blocks of matter, every process of observation causes a major disturbance' (Heisenberg 1972, p. 126), and that it is impossible to describe an objective world because the observer always changes the observed. However, the concerns of metafiction are even more complex than this. For while Heisenberg believed one could at least describe, if not a *picture* of nature, then a picture of one's *relation* to nature, metafiction shows the uncertainty even of this process. How is it possible to 'describe' anything? The metafictionist is highly conscious of a basic dilemma: if he or she sets out to 'represent' the world, he or she realizes fairly soon that the world, as such, cannot be 'represented'. In literary fiction it is, in fact, possible only to 'represent' the *discourses* of that world. Yet, if one attempts to

analyse a set of linguistic relationships using those same relationships as the instruments of analysis, language soon becomes a
'prisonhouse' from which the possibility of escape is remote.
Metafication sets out to explore this dilemma.

The linguist L. Hjelmslev developed the term 'metalanguage'
(Hjelmslev 1961). He defined it as a language which, instead of
referring to non-linguistic events, situations or objects in the
world, refers to *another* language: it is a language which takes
another language as its object. Saussure's distinction between
the signifier and the signified is relevant here. The signifier is the
sound-image of the word or its shape on the page; the signified is
the concept evoked by the word. A metalanguage is a language
that functions as a signifier to *another language*, and this other
language thus becomes its signified.[1]

In novelistic practice, this results in writing which consistently displays its conventionality, which explicity and overtly
lays bare its condition of artifice, and which thereby explores the
problematic relationship between life and fiction – both the fact
that 'all the world is not of course a stage' and 'the crucial ways
in which it isn't' (Goffman 1974, p. 53). The 'other' language
may be either the registers of everyday discourse or, more usually, the 'language' of the literary system itself, including the conventions of the novel as a whole or particular forms of that genre.

Metafiction may concern itself, then, with particular conventions of the novel, to display the process of their construction
(for example, John Fowles's use of the 'omniscient author'
convention in *The French Lieutenant's Woman* (1969). It may, often
in the form of parody, comment on a specific work or fictional
mode (for example, John Gardner's *Grendel* (1971), which
retells, and thus comments on, the *Beowulf* story from the point
of view of the monster; or John Hawkes's *The Lime Twig* (1961),
which constitutes both an example and a critique of the popular
thriller. Less centrally metafictional, but still displaying 'meta'
features, are fictions like Richard Brautigan's *Trout Fishing in
America* (1967). Such novels attempt to create alternative linguistic structures or fictions which merely *imply* the old forms by
encouraging the reader to draw on his or her knowledge of
traditional literary conventions when struggling to construct a
meaning for the new text.

Metafiction and the novel tradition

I would argue that metafictional practice has become particularly prominent in the fiction of the last twenty years. However, to draw exclusively on contemporary fiction would be misleading, for, although the *term* 'metafiction' might be new, the *practice* is as old (if not older) than the novel itself. What I hope to establish during the course of this book is that metafiction is a tendency or function inherent in *all* novels. This form of fiction is worth studying not only because of its contemporary emergence but also because of the insights it offers into both the representational nature of all fiction and the literary history of the novel as genre. By studying metafiction, one is, in effect, studying that which gives the novel its identity.

Certainly more scholarly ink has been spilt over attempts to define the novel than perhaps for any other literary genre. The novel notoriously defies definition. Its instability in this respect is part of its 'definition': the language of fiction appears to spill over into, and merge with, the instabilities of the real world, in a way that a five-act tragedy or a fourteen-line sonnet clearly does not. Metafiction flaunts and exaggerates and thus exposes the foundations of this instability: the fact that novels are constructed through a continuous assimilation of everyday historical forms of communication. There is no one privileged 'language of fiction'. There are the languages of memoirs, journals, diaries, histories, conversational registers, legal records, journalism, documentary. These languages compete for privilege. They question and relativize each other to such an extent that the 'language of fiction' is always, if often covertly, self-conscious.

Mikhail Bakhtin has referred to this process of relativization as the 'dialogic' potential of the novel. Metafiction simply makes this potential explicit and in so doing foregrounds the essential mode of all fictional language. Bakhtin defines as overtly 'dialogic' those novels that introduce a 'semantic direction into the word which is diametrically opposed to its original direction. . . . the word becomes the arena of conflict between two voices' (Bakhtin 1973, p. 106). In fact, given its close relation to everyday forms of discourse, the language of fiction is *always* to some extent dialogic. The novel assimilates a variety of discourses (representations of speech, forms of narrative) – discourses that *always* to some extent question and relativize each other's authority. Realism, often regarded as the classic fictional mode, paradoxically functions by suppressing this dialogue. The conflict of languages and voices is apparently resolved in realistic fiction through their subordination to the dominant 'voice' of the omniscient, godlike author. Novels which Bakhtin refers to as 'dialogic' resist such resolution. Metafiction *displays* and *rejoices in* the impossibility of such a resolution and thus clearly reveals the basic identity of the novel as genre.

Metafictional novels tend to be constructed on the principle of a fundamental and sustained opposition: the construction of a fictional illusion (as in traditional realism) and the laying bare of that illusion. In other words, the lowest common denominator of metafiction is simultaneously to create a fiction and to make a statement about the creation of that fiction. The two processes are held together in a formal tension which breaks down the distinctions between 'creation' and 'criticism' and merges them into the concepts of 'interpretation' and 'deconstruction'.

Although this oppositional process is to some extent present in all fiction, and particularly likely to emerge during 'crisis' periods in the literary history of the genre (see Chapter 3), its prominence in the contemporary novel is unique. The historical period we are living through has been singularly uncertain, insecure, self-questioning and culturally pluralistic. Contemporary fiction clearly reflects this dissatisfaction with, and breakdown of, traditional values. Previously, as in the case of nineteenth-century realism, the forms of fiction derived from a firm belief in a commonly experienced, objectively existing world of history. Modernist fiction, written in the earlier part of this century, responded to the initial loss of belief in such a world. Novels like Virginia Woolf's *To the Lighthouse* (1927) or James Joyce's *Ulysses* (1922) signalled the first widespread, overt emergence in the novel of a sense of fictitiousness: 'a sense that any attempt to represent reality could only produce selective perspectives, fictions, that is, in an epistemological, not merely in the conventional literary, sense' (Pfeifer 1978, p. 61).

Contemporary metafictional writing is both a response and a contribution to an even more thoroughgoing sense that reality or history are provisional: no longer a world of eternal verities but a series of constructions, artifices, impermanent structures. The materialist, positivist and empiricist world-view on which realistic fiction is premised no longer exists. It is hardly surprising, therefore, that more and more novelists have come to question and reject the forms that correspond to this ordered reality (the well-made plot, chronological sequence, the authoritative omniscient author, the rational connection between what characters 'do' and what they 'are', the causal connection between 'surface' details and the 'deep', 'scientific laws' of existence).

Why are they saying such awful things about it?

This rejection has inevitably entailed, however, a good deal of writerly and critical confusion. There has been paranoia, on the part of both novelists *and* critics for whom the exhaustion and rejection of realism is synonymous with the exhaustion and rejection of the novel itself. Thus B. S. Johnson bursts into (or out of?) *Albert Angelo* (1964) with the words which preface this chapter, 'Fuck all this lying'. His comment serves in the novel as much to voice a paranoid fear that his audience will misinterpret his fiction by reading it according to expectations based on the tradition of the realistic novel, as to demonstrate the artificiality of fictional form through a controlled metafictional discourse. At the end of the book he asserts:

> a page is an area on which I place my signs I consider to communicate most clearly what I have to convey . . . therefore I employ within the pocket of my publisher and the patience of my printer, typographical techniques beyond the arbitrary and constricting limits of the conventional novel. To dismiss such techniques as gimmicks or to refuse to take them seriously is crassly to miss the point.
>
> (*Albert Angelo*, p. 176)

It reads rather like an anticipation of a hostile review. A similar defensiveness about the role of the novelist appears in Donald Barthelme's obsession with *dreck*, the detritus of modern civilization.[2] It is expressed through John Barth's characters who – as much in the style of Sartre as in that of Sterne – 'die, telling themselves stories in the dark', desperately attempting to construct identities which can only dissolve into metalingual mutterings (*Lost in the Funhouse* (1968), p. 95). Extreme defensive strategies are common. Kurt Vonnegut's *Breakfast of Champions* (1973) is written to express the sense of absurdity produced by its author's paradoxical realization that 'I have no culture', and that 'I can't live without a culture anymore'; p. 15). Attempts at precise linguistic description continually break down. Crude diagrams replace language in order to express the poverty of the 'culture' which is available through representations of 'assholes', 'underpants' and 'beefburgers'.

The strategy of this novel is to invert the science-fiction convention whereby humans are depicted attempting to comprehend the processes of an alien world. Here, contemporary American society *is* the 'alien world'. Vonnegut defamiliarizes the world that his readers take for granted, through the technique of employing an ex-Earthling narrator who is now living on a different planet and has set out to 'explain' Earth to his fellow inhabitants. The defamiliarization has more than a satiric function, however. It reveals Vonnegut's own despairing recognition of the sheer impossibility of providing a critique of commonly accepted cultural forms of representation, from *within* those very modes of representation.

What is the novelist to do? Here the 'naïve' narrative voice, apparently oblivious of all our liberal value-systems and moral codes, reveals through its defamiliarizing effect their often *illiberal* and *amoral* assumptions and consequences. Beneath the fooling with representations of cows as beefburgers, however, lurks a desperate sense of the possible redundancy and irrelevance of the artist, so apparent in Vonnegut's *Slaughterhouse-Five* (1969). Indeed, Philip Roth, the American novelist, has written:

The American writer in the middle of the twentieth century has his hands full in trying to understand, describe, and then make credible much of American reality. It stupefies, it sickens, it infuriates, and finally it is even a kind of embarrassment to one's own meagre imagination. The actuality is continually outdoing our talents.

(Quoted in Bradbury 1977, p. 34)

In turning away from 'reality', however, and back to a re-examination of fictional form, novelists have discovered a surprising way out of their dilemmas and paranoia. Metafictional deconstruction has not only provided novelists and their readers with a better understanding of the fundamental structures of narrative; it has also offered extremely accurate models for understanding the contemporary experience of the world as a construction, an artifice, a web of interdependent semiotic systems. The paranoia that permeates the metafictional writing of the sixties and seventies is therefore slowly giving way to celebration, to the discovery of new forms of the fantastic, fabulatory extravaganzas, magic realism (Salman Rushdie, Gabriel García Márquez, Clive Sinclair, Graham Swift, D. M. Thomas, John Irving). Novelists and critics alike have come to realize that a moment of crisis can also be seen as a moment of recognition: recognition that, although the assumptions about the novel based on an extension of a nineteenth-century realist view of the world may no longer be viable, the novel itself is positively flourishing.

Despite this renewed optimism, however, it is still the case that the uncertain, self-reflexive nature of experimental metafiction will leave it open to critical attacks. Yet metafiction is simply flaunting what is true of *all* novels: their 'outstanding freedom to choose' (Fowles 1971, p. 46). It is this instability, openness and flexibility which has allowed the novel remarkably to survive and adapt to social change for the last 300 years. In the face of the political, cultural and technological upheavals in society since the Second World War, however, its lack of a fixed identity has now left the novel vulnerable.

Hence critics have discussed the 'crisis of the novel' and the 'death of the novel'. Instead of recognizing the *positive* aspects of fictional self-consciousness, they have tended to see such literary behaviour as a form of the self-indulgence and decadence characteristic of the exhaustion of any artistic form or genre.

Could it not be argued instead that metafictional writers, highly conscious of the problems of artistic legitimacy, simply sensed a need for the novel to theorize about itself? Only in this way might the genre establish an identity and validity within a culture apparently hostile to its printed, linear narrative and conventional assumptions about 'plot', 'character', 'authority' and 'representation'. The traditional fictional quest has thus been transformed into a quest for fictionality.

Metafiction and the contemporary avant-garde

This search has been further motivated by novelists' responses to another feature of contemporary cultural life: the absence of a clearly defined avant-garde 'movement'. The existence of an unprecedented cultural pluralism has meant that post-modernist writers are not confronted with the same clear-cut oppositions as modernist writers were. An innovation in a literary form cannot establish itself as a new direction unless a sense of shared aims and objectives develops among experimental writers. This has been slow to take shape in recent years. An argument originally advanced by Lionel Trilling in *Beyond Culture* (Trilling 1966) and reiterated by Gerald Graff has suggested one reason for this: that the unmasking of the 'hypocritical bourgeois belief in the material and moral progress of civilization' (Graff 1975, p. 308) has been so thoroughly accomplished by modernism that the creative tension produced by opposing this 'bourgeois belief' is no longer clearly available the novelist.

In eighteenth- and nineteenth-century fiction, the individual is always finally integrated into the social structure (usually through family relationships, marriage, birth or the ultimate dissolution of death). In modernist fiction the struggle for personal autonomy can be continued only through *opposition* to existing social institutions and conventions. This struggle necessarily involves individual alienation and often ends with mental dissolution. The power structures of *contemporary* society are, however, more diverse and more effectively concealed or mystified, creating greater problems for the post-modernist novelist in identifying and then representing the object of 'opposition'.

Metafictional writers have found a solution to this by turning inwards to their own medium of expression, in order to examine the relationship between fictional form and social reality. They have come to focus on the notion that 'everyday' language endorses and sustains such power structures through a continuous process of naturalization whereby forms of oppression are constructed in apparently 'innocent' representations. The literary-fictional equivalent of this 'everyday' language of 'common sense' is the language of the traditional novel: the conventions of realism. Metafiction sets up an opposition, not to ostensibly 'objective' facts in the 'real' world, but to the language of the realistic novel which has sustained and endorsed such a view of reality.

The metafictional novel thus situates its resistance *within* the form of the novel itself. Saussure distinguished between *langue* and *parole*: between the language system (a set of rules) and any act of individual utterance that takes place within this system. Each metafictional novel self-consciously sets its individual *parole* against the *langue* (the codes and conventions) of the novel tradition. Ostentatiously 'literary' language and conventions are paraded, are set against the fragments of various cultural codes, not because there is nothing left to talk about, but because the formal structures of these literary conventions provide a statement about the dissociation between, on the one hand, the genuinely felt sense of crisis, alienation and oppression in contemporary society and, on the other, the continuance of traditional literary forms like realism which are no longer adequate vehicles for the mediation of this experience. Metafiction thus converts what it sees as the negative values of outworn literary conventions into the basis of a potentially constructive social criticism. It suggests, in fact, that there may be as much to be learnt from setting the mirror of art up to its own linguistic or representational structures as from directly setting it up to a hypothetical 'human nature' that somehow exists as an essence outside historical systems of articulation.

The problem facing writers who attempt authentically to represent conditions of rapid social change is that they may themselves produce works of art which are ephemeral and even trivial. In the present situation 'even a single work will be sufficient grounds for declaring a style finished, exhausted' (Rochberg 1971, p. 73). The practitioners of so-called 'aleatory art' (which attempts to be totally random in order to suggest the chaotic, frenetic and colliding surfaces of contemporary technological society) are open to these charges. Literary texts tend to function by preserving a balance between the unfamiliar (the innovatory) and the familiar (the conventional or traditional). Both are necessary because some degree of redundancy is essential for any message to be committed to memory. Redundancy is provided for in literary texts through the presence of familiar conventions. Experimental fiction of the aleatory variety eschews such redundancy by simply ignoring the conventions of literary tradition. Such texts set out to resist the normal processes of reading, memory and understanding, but without redundancy, texts are read and forgotten. They cannot unite to form a literary 'movement' because they exist only at the moment of reading.

The metafictional response to the problem of how to represent impermanence and a sense of chaos, in the permanent and ordered terms of literature, has had a much more significant influence on the development of the novel as genre. Aleatory writing might imitate the experience of living in the contemporary world, but it fails to offer any of the comfort traditionally supplied by literary fiction through a 'sense of an ending' (Kermode 1966). Metafiction, however, offers both innovation *and* familiarity through the individual reworking and undermining of familiar conventions.

Aleatory writing simply responds with a reply in kind to the pluralistic, hyperactive multiplicity of styles that constitute the surfaces of present-day culture. What is mainly asserted in such novels is an anarchic individualism, a randomness designed to represent an avoidance of social control by stressing the impossibility of easily categorizing it or assimilating the reader to familiar structures of communication. An argument sometimes proposed to justify the strategies of such fictions is that they are 'radical' because they rupture the conventional linguistic contracts that certify and/or disguise orthodox social practices (as realism, for example, certifies concepts like 'eternal human nature' or the assumption that authority as manifested through the omniscient author is somehow free of both gender distinctions and of historically constructed and provisional moral values). Such novels supposedly expose the way in which these social practices are constructed through the language of oppressive ideologies, by refusing to allow the reader the role of passive consumer or any means of arriving at a 'total' interpretation of the text.

Although it is true that much of this should undoubtedly be the task of experimental fiction, it does seem questionable whether, for many readers, so-called 'aleatory writing' is going to accomplish all of this. Novels like John Fowles's *The French Lieutenant's Woman* or Robert Coover's *Pricksongs and Descants* (1969), though apparently less 'radical', are in the long run likely to be more successful. Both are metafictional novels in that they employ parody self-consciously. Both take as their 'object' languages the structures of nineteenth-century realism and of historical romance or of fairy-tales. The parody of these 'languages' functions to defamiliarize such structures by setting up various counter-techniques to undermine the authority of the omniscient author, of the closure of the 'final' ending, of the definitive interpretation. Although the reader is thereby distanced from the language, the literary conventions and, ultimately, from conventional ideologies, the defamiliarization proceeds from an extremely familiar base. Such novels can thus initially be comprehended through the old structures, and can therefore be enjoyed and remain in the consciousness of a wide readership which is given a far more active role in the construction of the 'meaning' of the text than is provided either in contemporary realist novels or in novels which convert their readers into frenetic human word-processors, and which 'last' only as long as it takes to read them.

The mirror up to art: metafiction and its varieties

It remains, within this introductory chapter, briefly to examine some alternative definitions of self-conscious writing. These similar modes have been variously termed 'the introverted novel', 'the anti-novel', 'irrealism', 'surfiction', 'the self-begetting novel', 'fabulation'.[3] All, like 'metafiction', imply a fiction that self-consciously reflects upon its own structure as language; all offer different perspectives on the same process. But the terms shift the emphasis in different ways. The 'self-begetting novel', for example, is described as an 'account usually first person, of the development of a character to a point at which he is able to take up and compose the novel we have just finished reading' (Kellman 1976, p. 1245). The emphasis is on the development of the narrator, on the modernist concern of *consciousness* rather than the post-modernist one of *fictionality* (as in, for example, André Gide's *The Counterfeiters* (1925)).

The entry of the narrator into the text is also a defining feature of what has been called 'surfiction'. Raymond Federman's book of that name discusses the mode in terms of overt narratorial intrusion so that, as in the 'self-begetting novel', the focus appears to be on the ironist him/herself rather than on the overt and covert levels of the ironic text. Telling as individual invention, spontaneous fabrication at the expense of external reality or literary tradition, is emphasized rather than what has been stressed above: metafiction's continuous involvement in – and mediation of – reality through linguistic structures and pre-existent texts.

As defined here, of course, metafictional writing may include all or some of the strategies that critics have discussed in the terms that have been mentioned. Different categories, in fact, often compete for the same fictional texts: John Barth's *Lost in the Funhouse* (1968) is clearly 'self-begetting', 'surfictional' *and* 'metafictional'. As I have argued, metafiction is not so much a sub-genre of the novel as a tendency *within* the novel which operates through exaggeration of the tensions and oppositions inherent in all novels: of frame and frame-break, of technique and counter-technique, of construction and deconstruction of illusion. Metafiction thus expresses overtly what William H. Gass has argued is the dilemma of all art:

> In every art two contradictory impulses are in a state of Manichean war: the impulse to communicate and so to treat the medium of communication as a means and the impulse to

make an artefact out of the materials and so to treat the
medium as an end.   (Gass 1970)

The expression of this tension is present in much contemporary
writing but it is the *dominant* function in the texts defined here as
metafictional.

The metafictions of Jorge Luis Borges and Vladimir Nabokov
illustrate this point. In some of their work – Borges' *Labyrinths*
(1964) and Nabokov's *Pale Fire* (1962), for example – fiction
explicitly masquerades as formalized critical interpretation. In
all their work, however, as in all other metafiction, there is a
more complex *implicit* interdependence of levels than this. The
reader is always presented with embedded strata which contradict the presuppositions of the strata immediately above or
below. The fictional *content* of the story is continually reflected
by its *formal* existence as text, and the existence of that text
within a world viewed in terms of 'textuality'. Brian McHale
has suggested that such contradictions are essentially *ontological*
(posing questions about the nature and existence of reality) and
are therefore characteristically post-modernist. He sees as modernist those *epistemological* contradictions which question how
we can know a reality whose existence is finally not in doubt
(McHale, forthcoming).

Borges' imaginary kingdom Tlön, discovered by the 'fortun-
ate conjunction of a mirror and an encyclopaedia', is a post-
modernist world. It is twice a fiction because it is suggested that,
before its invention by Borges, it has already been invented by a
secret society of idealists including Bishop Berkeley, and both,
of course, are finally dependent upon the conventions of the
short story (*Labyrinths*, p. 27). The fact that this 'imaginary'
world can take over the 'real' one emphasizes more than the
epistemological uncertainty of both of them (which would be the
aim of the 'self-begetting novel'). 'Tlön Uqbar Orbis Tertius',
the story, is about a story that invents an imaginary world, and
it primarily and self-consciously *is* a story which, like all stories,
invents an imaginary world. It implies that human beings can
only ever achieve a metaphor for reality, another layer of
'interpretation'. (Borges' story 'Funes the Memorias' (1964)
shows that this need not be cause for despair, for if indeed we

could not create these metaphorical images then we would all surely become insane.)

Metafictional novels (unlike 'surfiction' or 'the self-begetting novel') thus reject the traditional figure of the author as a transcendental imagination fabricating, through an ultimately monologic discourse, structures of order which will replace the forgotten material text of the world. They show not only that the 'author' is a concept produced through previous and existing literary and social texts but that what is generally taken to be 'reality' is also constructed and mediated in a similar fashion. 'Reality' is to this extent 'fictional' and can be understood through an appropriate 'reading' process.

Also rejected is the displacement of 'historical man' by 'structural man' advocated by Robert Scholes as the basis of what he calls 'fabulation' (Scholes 1975). David Lodge has pointed out that 'history may be in a philosophical sense, a fiction, but it does not feel like that when we miss a train or somebody starts a war'.[4] As novel readers, we look to fiction to offer us cognitive functions, to locate us within everyday as well as within philosophical paradigms, to explain the historical world as well as offer some formal comfort and certainty. Scholes argues that the empirical has lost all validity and that a collusion between the philosophic and the mythic in the form of 'ethically controlled fantasy' is the only authentic mode for fiction (Scholes 1967, p. 11). However, metafiction offers the recognition, not that the everyday has ceased to matter, but that its formulation through social and cultural codes brings it closer to the philosophical and mythic than was once assumed.

A brief comparison of two self-conscious novels, one obviously 'metafictional', the other more obviously 'fabulatory', shows how metafiction explores the concept of fictionality through an opposition between the construction and the breaking of illusion, while fabulation reveals instead what Christine Brooke-Rose (1980) has referred to as a reduced tension between technique and counter-technique: a 'stylization' which enables other voices to be *assimilated*, rather than presenting a conflict of voices.

Muriel Spark's *metafictional* novels lay bare the process of imposing form upon contingent matter through the discursive

organization of 'plot'. She can, however, as David Lodge has
said of Joyce, afford her metaphoric flights because of the
stability of her metonymic base (Lodge 1977a, p. 111). She uses
her 'flights', in fact, to comment on the very paradigms that they
are in the process of constructing (this embedding of strata, of
course, being fundamental to metafiction). In *Not to Disturb*
(1971), for example, this highly obtrusive simile describes a
storm:

> Meanwhile the lightning which strikes the clump of elms so
> that the two friends huddled there are killed instantly without
> pain, zigzags across the lawns, illuminating the lily-pond and
> the sunken rose garden like a self-stricken flash photo-
> grapher, and like a zip-fastener ripped from its garment by a
> sexual maniac.
>
> (p. 86)

This appears to be a piece of highly stylized descriptive prose
marked particularly by the appearance of extremely bizarre
metaphors. To this extent it is very similar to Richard Brautigan's *fabulatory* novel, *Trout Fishing in America* (1967), which is
full of similar metaphorical constructions where the extreme
polarity of vehicle and tenor implicitly reminds the reader of the
way in which metaphor constructs an image of reality by
connecting apparently quite disparate objects. In this novel, for
example, trout are described waiting in streams 'like airplane
tickets' (p. 78), and the reader's imagination is stretched
throughout by the incongruity of the comparisons. The novel is
a celebration of the creative imagination: it is a 'fabulation'.

In the Spark example, however, there is a further, more
subtle function that is part of a sustained metafictional display;
for the vehicle of the metaphor is explicitly related to what is
happening at the contiguously unfolding level of the story. A
group of entrepreneurial and enterprising servants have
arranged the filming of the last moments of an eternal triangle of
superannuated aristocrats. The servants know their masters are
going to die and also know how to capitalize on their deaths.
Aristocratic scandals provide excellent material for media sensationalism. The photographer and the zip fastener (which the
mentally deficient aristocratic son is continually attempting to

rip off in the excitement of his intermittent sexual energy) are important elements in the plot being constructed by the novelist (who also, as in the example, arranges appropriate climatic conditions) and, of course, by the characters. The reader is alerted to the way in which the explicitly artificial construction of these connections fits in with the larger designs of the novelist playing God. The elements at the metaphorical level of the construction break down not into 'natural' or randomly chosen components, but to another level of artifice: the level of the 'plot'. The reader is thus reminded that pure contingency in novels is always an illusion, although the lowest level of the artifice (what the Russian formalist Boris Tomashevsky has referred to as realistic motivation; see Lemon and Reis 1965, pp. 61–99) is assumed to be reality. Thus not only do the characters in this novel play roles, 'fictionalize' in terms of the *content* of the plot; they too are 'fictionalized', created, through the *formal construction* of the plot.

Metafiction explicitly lays bare the conventions of realism; it does not ignore or abandon them. Very often realistic conventions supply the 'control' in metafictional texts, the norm or background against which the experimental strategies can foreground themselves. More obviously, of course, this allows for a stable level of readerly familiarity, without which the ensuing dislocations might be either totally meaningless or so outside the normal modes of literary or non-literary communication that they cannot be committed to memory (the problem, already discussed, of much contemporary 'aleatory' writing). Metafiction, then, does not abandon 'the real world' for the narcissistic pleasures of the imagination. What it does is to re-examine the conventions of realism in order to discover – through its own self-reflection – a fictional form that is culturally relevant and comprehensible to contemporary readers. In showing us how literary fiction creates its imaginary worlds, metafiction helps us to understand how the reality we live day by day is similarly constructed, similarly 'written'.

'Metafiction' is thus an elastic term which covers a wide range of fictions. There are those novels at one end of the spectrum which take fictionality as a theme to be explored (and in this sense would include the 'self-begetting novel'), as in the work of Iris Murdoch or Jerzy Kosinski, whose formal self-consciousness is limited. At the centre of this spectrum are those texts that manifest the symptoms of formal and ontological insecurity but allow their deconstructions to be finally recontextualized or 'naturalized' and given a total interpretation (which constitute, therefore, a 'new realism'), as in the work of John Fowles or E. L. Doctorow. Finally, at the furthest extreme (which would include 'fabulation') can be placed those fictions that, in rejecting realism more thoroughly, posit the world as a fabrication of competing semiotic systems which never correspond to material conditions, as in the work of Gilbert Sorrentino, Raymond Federman or Christine Brooke-Rose.

Much British fiction fits into the first half of the spectrum, though problematically, and much American fiction into the other half, though with the same proviso. The novelist at either end, however – in confronting the problem that, 'whether or not he makes peace with realism, he must somehow cope with reality' (Dickinson 1975, p. 372) – has acknowledged the fact that this 'reality' is no longer the one mediated by nineteenth-century novelists and experienced by nineteenth-century readers. Indeed, it could be argued that, far from 'dying', the novel has reached a mature recognition of its existence as *writing*, which can only ensure its continued viability in and relevance to a contemporary world which is similarly beginning to gain awareness of precisely how its values and practices are constructed and legitimized.

2

Literary self-consciousness: developments

Modernism and post-modernism: the redefinition of self-consciousness

Metafiction is a mode of writing within a broader cultural movement often referred to as post-modernism. The metafictional writer John Barth has expressed a common feeling about the term 'post-modernism' as 'awkward and faintly epigonic, suggestive less of a vigorous or even interesting new direction in the old art of storytelling than of something anticlimactic, feebly following a very hard act to follow' (Barth 1980, p. 66). Post-modernism can be seen to exhibit the same sense of crisis and loss of belief in an external authoritative system of order as that which prompted modernism. Both affirm the constructive powers of the mind in the face of apparent phenomenal chaos. Modernist self-consciousness, however, though it may draw attention to the aesthetic construction of the text, does *not* 'systematically flaunt its own condition of artifice' (Alter 1975a, p. x) in the manner of contemporary metafiction.

Modernism only occasionally displays features typical of post-modernism: the over-obtrusive, visibly inventing narrator (as in Barth's *Lost in the Funhouse* (1968), Robert Coover's *Pricksongs and Descants* (1969)); ostentatious typographic experiment (B. S. Johnson's *Travelling People* (1963), Raymond Federman's *Double or Nothing* (1971)); explicit dramatization of the

reader (Italo Calvino's *If on a Winter's Night a Traveller* (1979));
Chinese-box structures (Doris Lessing's *The Golden Notebook*
(1962), John Barth's *Chimera* (1972)); incantatory and absurd
lists (Donald Barthelme's *Snow White* (1967), Gabriel Josipovici's *The Inventory* (1968)); over-systematized or overtly arbitrarily arranged structural devices (Walter Abish's *Alphabetical
Africa* (1974)); total breakdown of temporal and spatial organization of narrative (B. S. Johnson's 'A Few Selected Sentences' (1973)); infinite regress (Beckett's *Watt* (1953)); dehumanization of character, parodic doubles, obtrusive proper
names (Pynchon's *Gravity's Rainbow* (1973)); self-reflexive images (Nabokov's mirrors, acrostics, mazes); critical discussions
of the story within the story (Fowles's 'The Enigma' (1974),
Barth's *Sabbatical* (1982)); continuous undermining of specific
fictional conventions (Muriel Spark's quasi-omniscient author,
Fowles's very un-Victorian ending in *The French Lieutenant's
Woman* (1969)); use of popular genres (Richard Brautigan's *A
Confederate General from Big Sur* (1964), Vonnegut's *Slaughterhouse-Five* (1969)); and explicit parody of previous texts whether
literary or non-literary (Gilbert Sorrentino's *Mulligan Stew*
(1979), Alan Burns's *Babel* (1969)).

In all of these what is foregrounded is the writing of the text as
the most fundamentally problematic aspect of that text.
Although metafiction is just one form of post-modernism, nearly all contemporary experimental writing displays *some* explicitly metafictional strategies. Any text that draws the reader's
attention to its process of construction by frustrating his or her
conventional expectations of meaning and closure problema-
tizes more or less explicitly the ways in which narrative codes –
whether 'literary' or 'social' – artificially construct apparently
'real' and imaginary worlds in the terms of particular ideologies
while presenting these as transparently 'natural' and 'eternal'.

In 1945 Joseph Frank explained the self-referential quality of
modernist literature in these terms:

Since the primary reference of any word group is to something inside the poem itself, language in modern poetry is
really reflexive . . . instead of the instinctive and immediate
reference of words and word groups to the objects and events

they symbolize, and the construction of meaning from the
sequence of these references, modern poetry asks its readers
to suspend the process of individual reference temporarily
until the entire pattern of internal references can be
apprehended as a unity.

(Frank 1958, p. 73)

In short, self-reflexiveness in modernist texts generates 'spatial
form'. With realist writing the reader has the illusion of constructing an interpretation by referring the words of the text to
objects in the real world. However, with texts like T. S. Eliot's
The Waste Land (1922), in order to construct a satisfactory
interpretation of the poem, the reader must follow the complex
web of cross-references and repetitions of words and images
which function independently of, or in addition to, the narrative
codes of causality and sequence. The reader becomes aware
that 'meaning' is constructed primarily through internal *verbal*
relationships, and the poem thus appears to achieve a verbal
autonomy: a 'spatial form'. Such organization persists in contemporary metafictional texts, but merely as *one* aspect of
textual self-reflexivity. Indeed, 'spatial form' may *itself* function
in these fictions as the object of self-conscious attention (for a
discussion of this aspect of Kurt Vonnegut's *Slaughterhouse-Five*,
see Chapter 5).

Post-modernism clearly does not involve the modernist concern with the mind as itself the basis of an aesthetic, ordered at a
profound level and revealed to consciousness at isolated
'epiphanic' moments. At the end of Virginia Woolf's *To the
Lighthouse* (1927), for example, Lily Briscoe suddenly perceives
a higher (or deeper) order in things as she watches the boat
return. Her realization is translated, directly and overtly, into
aesthetic terms. Returning to her canvas, with intensity she
draws the final line: 'It was finished. Yes she thought laying
down her brush in extreme fatigue, I have had my vision' (p.
320). A post-modern 'line' is more likely to imitate that drawn
by Tristram Shandy to represent the plot of his 'life and times'
(resembling a diagram of the formation of an oxbow lake). In
fact, if post-modernism shares some of the philosophies of
modernism, its formal techniques seem often to have originated

from novels like *Tristram Shandy* (1760), *Don Quixote* (1604) or *Tom Jones* (1749).

For Sterne, as for contemporary writers, the mind is not a perfect aestheticizing instrument. It is not free, and it is as much constructed out of, as constructed with, language. The substitution of a purely metaphysical system (as in the case of Proust) or mythical analogy (as with Joyce and Eliot) cannot be accepted by the metafictionist as final structures of authority and meaning. Contemporary reflexivity implies an awareness both of language *and* metalanguage, of consciousness *and* writing.

B. S. Johnson's 'A Few Selected Sentences', for example, is precisely what its title suggests: a series of fragments taken from a wide variety of discursive practices (ranging from a sixteenth-century description of the cacao fruit to absurd warnings) which, although resisting final totalization, can be arranged into a number of conventional narratives. The most obvious of these is a comment on what we are doing as we read: constructing a detective story. The style is reminiscent of Eliot's technique of fragmentation and montage in *The Waste Land*, but there the connections are present despite the fragmentary surface, to be recovered through the mythic consciousness as the reader partakes in the modern equivalent of the Grail search. The fragments which Johnson has shored against his ruins are not at all explicable by any such *a priori* transcendental system, only by his readers' knowledge of the conventions of stories. There is no longer a deep, structured collective unconscious to be relied upon, only the heavily italicized and multi-coded 'Life' with which the story ends (p. 80).

Whereas loss of order for the modernist led to the belief in its recovery at a deeper level of the mind, for metafictional writers the most fundamental assumption is that composing a novel is basically no different from composing or constructing one's 'reality'. Writing itself rather than consciousness becomes the main object of attention. Questioning not only the notion of the novelist as God, through the flaunting of the author's godlike role, but also the authority of consciousness, of the mind, metafiction establishes the categorization of the world through the arbitrary system of language. The modernist writer whose style fits closest with this essentially post-modernist mode of writing is, of course, James Joyce. Even in *A Portrait of the Artist as a Young Man* (1916), the epiphanic moments are usually connected with a self-reflexive response to language itself. The word 'foetus', for example, scratched on a desk, forces upon Stephen's consciousness a recognition of his whole 'monstrous way of life' (pp. 90–2).

Ulysses (1922) goes further in showing 'reality' to be a consequence of 'style'. However, despite parody, stylization and imitation of non-literary discourses, there is no overtly self-referential voice which systematically establishes, as the main focus of the novel, the problematic relationship of language and 'reality'. The only strictly metafictional line is Molly's 'Oh Jamesy let me up out of this Pooh' (p. 691), though there are many inherently self-conscious devices now widely used by metafictional writers, and the 'Oxen of the Sun' section is, of course, an extended piece of literary pastiche. Each of the parodies of literary styles in this section presents a direct and problematical relationship between style and content which draws attention to the fact that language is not simply a set of empty forms filled with meaning, but that it actually dictates and circumscribes what can be said and therefore what can be perceived. When a discussion of contraception, for example, creeps into the parody of the language of courtly love, the reader is made to see contraception in a new light. The realities of procreation in the twentieth century are thrown into a different perspective through their discussion within the linguistic parameters of the medieval world.

Ulysses has eighteen chapters and eighteen main styles. B. S. Johnson's *Travelling People* (1963), overtly both Shandyan and Joycean, has nine chapters and styles. Style is explicitly explored here in terms of negativity: how it represents certain aspects of experience only by excluding others. The novel begins by parodying the opening of *Tom Jones*, with Johnson setting out his 'bill of fare' and explaining that the style of each chapter should spring from its subject matter. Each shift of style is further accompanied by a Fieldingesque chapter heading, which, through its equally vacuous generality in Johnson's text, undermines the attempt of such verbal signposts to be comprehensive. The introduction, headings and 'interludes' com-

plement the Joycean stylistic shifts through which the characters, the rootless 'travelling people' of the contemporary world,
attempt to construct identities for themselves.

Henry, the protagonist, for example, is shown continually
stylizing his existence, distancing unpleasant realities such as
how many dogs are required to manufacture a certain amount
of glue by communicating the information to himself in the
language of a strident advertising slogan: 'See that your pet has
a happy home in Henry's glue' (p. 12). The reader is thus made
aware of how reality is *subjectively* constructed. But beyond this
essentially modernist perspective, the text reveals a post-
modernist concern with how it is itself *linguistically* constructed.
Through continuous narrative intrusion, the reader is reminded
that not only do characters verbally construct their own realities; they are themselves verbal constructions, *words* not *beings*.

It might seem that in its (to quote Flann O'Brien) 'self-
evident sham' (*At Swim-Two-Birds* (1939), p.25) metafiction has
merely reduced the complex stylistic manœuvres of modernism
to a set of crude statements about the relation of literary fictions
to the real world. The opening page of John Barth's *The Floating
Opera* (1956), for example, might appear in this light:

> It has always seemed to me in the novels that I've read now
> and then, that the authors are asking a great deal of their
> readers who start their stories furiously in the middle of
> things, rather than backing or sliding slowly into them. Such
> a plunge into someone else's life and world . . . has, it seems,
> little of pleasure in it. No, come along with me reader, and
> don't fear for your weak heart. Good heavens, how does one
> write a novel . . .

This seems a far cry from the plunge into the complex flow of
consciousness characteristic of the opening of modernist novels
such as *Ulysses* or *To the Lighthouse*. It is, in fact, much closer to
Sterne's establishment of the novelist as conversationalist, as
dependent on the reader for identity and sympathy. Thus
Tristram begs his reader, 'bear with me – and let me go on and
tell my story in my own way' (*Tristram Shandy*, p. 15). It also
signals the contemporary writer agonizing – like Sterne, like
Tristram – over the problem of beginnings but, unlike them,

with a new sophisticated narrative awareness that a story never has a 'real' beginning, can only ever begin arbitrarily, be recounted as plot. A 'story' cannot exist without a teller. The apparent *impersonality* of *histoire* is always finally *personal*, finally *discours*.[5]

The themes of Barth's novel in many ways resemble those of much modernist fiction. Its central character Todd realizes that existence cannot finally be explained in the terms of logical causality. There is no original 'source' of one's behaviour, whether one draws on psychological, environmental or physical evidence. The attempt to trace such a source is, in fact, doomed in precisely the way of Walter Shandy's encyclopaedia. The incompleteness which permeates everything in Tristram's account is here present, frustrating the modern concern to define reality in terms of a unified consciousness, a whole self. Thus Todd's modernist solipsism is continually undermined by the ironic and sometimes comic use of various Shandyan devices. In its recognition that the limits of one's language define the limits of one's self, metafiction breaks into solipsism by showing that the consciousness of Todd is here caught in a net not of its *own* making but of that of the *novelist* and, ultimately, that of the very public medium of *language*.

As Sartre argued in *Being and Nothingness* (1956), acts of consciousness have to be conscious of themselves, so that even when consciousness is focused on something else – when writing, for example – it must remain aware of itself on the edges of consciousness or the subject cannot continue to write. Modernism aimed at the impossible task of exploring pure consciousness. Metafiction has accepted Wittgenstein's notion that 'one thinks that one is tracing the outline of the thing's nature over and over again and one is merely tracing round the frame through which we look at it' (quoted in Josipovici 1977, p. 296).

Having differentiated briefly between the modes of literary self-consciousness characteristic of modernist and post-modernist writing, this chapter will now attempt to examine the concerns of contemporary metafiction in relation to some of the changes in the way in which reality is mediated and constructed by cultural theory and practice outside the strict domain of the 'literary'. Literature should not be analysed as a form of expression which simply sets up its own traditions and conventions totally apart from those that structure non-literary culture. If metafiction is to be seen as a positive stage in the development of the novel, then its relevance and sensitivity to the increasing and diverse manifestations of self-consciousness in the culture as a whole have to be established.

Two leading ideas in the field of sociology have been the notion of history/reality as a construct, and the idea of 'framing' as the activity through which it is constructed. Psychologists, sociologists and even economists have surely proved the tremendous importance of the serious possibilities of 'play'. Nevertheless it seems to be these aspects of metafictional writing that critics seize on to accuse it of ephemerality and irrelevance. This chapter aims to look at the ways in which metafictional techniques can be seen as a response to such non-literary cultural developments.

The analysis of frames: metafiction and frame-breaking

A frame may be defined as a 'construction, constitution, build; established order, plan, system . . . underlying support or essential substructure of anything' (*Oxford English Dictionary*). Modernism and post-modernism begin with the view that both the historical world and works of art are organized and perceived through such structures or 'frames'. Both recognize further that the distinction between 'framed' and 'unframed' cannot in the end be made. Everything is framed, whether in life or in novels. Ortega y Gasset, writing on modernism, pointed out, however, that 'not many people are capable of adjusting their perceptive apparatus to the pane and the transparency that is the work of art. Instead they look right through it and revel in the human reality with which the work deals' (Ortega y Gasset 1948, p. 31). Contemporary metafiction, in particular, foregrounds 'framing' as a problem, examining frame procedures in the construction of the real world and of novels. The first problem it poses, of course, is: what is a 'frame'? What is the 'frame' that separates reality from 'fiction'? Is it more than the front and back covers of a book, the rising and lowering of a curtain, the title and 'The End'?

Modernist texts begin by plunging in *in medias res* and end with the sense that nothing is finished, that life flows on. Metafictional novels often begin with an explicit discussion of the arbitrary nature of beginnings, of boundaries, as in Graham Greene's *The End of the Affair* (1951): 'A story has no beginning or end: arbitrarily one chooses that moment of experience from which to look back or from which to look ahead' (p. 7). They often end with a choice of endings. Or they may end with a sign of the impossibility of endings. Julio Cortázar's *Hopscotch* (1967) presents the reader with two 'books': the book can be read according to the order in which it is printed, or it can be read according to an alternative order presented to the reader in the 'conclusion', the apparent 'end' of the first order. The first 'book' is read up to chapter 56; the second 'book' begins at chapter 73 and covers the whole novel except for chapter 55. The final 'end' is now apparently in chapter 58, but, when the reader gets there, it is to discover that he or she should go back to chapter 131, and so on and on and on. The final chapter printed is chapter 155 (which directs the reader back to 123), so the last printed words are: 'Wait'll I finish my cigarette' (*Hopscotch*, p. 564). We are still waiting . . .

Alternatively, such novels may end with a gloss upon the archetypal fictional ending, the 'happily ever after'. John Barth's *Sabbatical* (1982) poses the question whether the ending of the events begins the writing, or the ending of the writing begins the events. Susan decides that they should 'begin it at the end and end at the beginning, so we can go on forever. Begin with our living happily ever after' (p. 365); but her author has decided: 'we commence as we would conclude, that they lived

Happily ever after, to the end of Fenwick and Susie . . .'

(p. 366)

Contemporary metafiction draws attention to the fact that life, as well as novels, is constructed through frames, and that it is finally impossible to know where one frame ends and another begins. Contemporary sociologists have argued along similar lines. Erving Goffman in *Frame Analysis* has suggested that there is no simple dichotomy 'reality/fiction':

When we decide that something is unreal, the real it isn't need not itself be very real, indeed, can just as well be a dramatization of events as the events themselves – or a rehearsal of the dramatization, or a painting of the rehearsal or a reproduction of the painting. Any of these latter can serve as the original of which something is a mere mock-up, leading one to think that which is sovereign is relationship – not substance.

(Goffman 1974, pp. 560–1)

Frames in life operate like conventions in novels: they facilitate action and involvement in a situation. Goffman defines frames early in his book:

I assume that definitions of a situation are built up in accordance with principles which govern events – at least social ones – and our subjective involvement in them; frame is the word I use to refer to such of these basic elements as I am able to identify.

(ibid., p. 67)

Analysis of frames is the analysis, in the above terms, of the organization of experience. When applied to fiction it involves analysis of the formal conventional organization of novels. What both Goffman and metafictional novels highlight through the foregrounding and analysis of framing activities is the extent to which we have become aware that neither historical experiences nor literary fictions are unmediated or unprocessed or non-linguistic or, as the modernists would have it, 'fluid' or 'random'. Frames are essential in all fiction. They become more perceptible as one moves from realist to modernist modes and are explicitly laid bare in metafiction.

In metafictional novels, obvious framing devices range from stories within stories (John Irving's *The World According to Garp* (1976)), characters reading about their own fictional lives (Calvino's *If on a Winter's Night a Traveller*) and self-consuming worlds or mutually contradictory situations (Coover's 'The Babysitter', 'The Magic Poker' (1971)). The concept of 'frame' includes Chinese-box structures which contest the reality of each individual 'box' through a nesting of narrators (Flann O'Brien's *At Swim-Two-Birds* (1939), John Barth's *Chimera* (1972)). Similar are so-called 'fictions of infinity' such as

Borges' 'Library of Babel', where 'In order to locate Book B, first consult Book C and so on *ad infinitum*' (*Labyrinths*, p. 84). Sometimes overt frames involve a confusion of ontological levels through the incorporation of visions, dreams, hallucinatory states and pictorial representations which are finally indistinct from the apparently 'real' (Alain Robbe-Grillet's *Dans le labyrinthe* (1959), Thomas Pynchon's *Gravity's Rainbow*, Doris Lessing's *The Memoirs of a Survivor* (1974) and *Briefing for a Descent into Hell* (1971)). Such infinities of texts within texts draw out the paradoxical relationship of 'framed' and 'unframed' and, in effect, of 'form' and 'content'. There is ultimately no distinction between 'framed' and 'unframed'. There are only levels of form. There is ultimately only 'content' perhaps, but it will never be discovered in a 'natural' unframed state.

One method of showing the function of literary conventions, of revealing their provisional nature, is to show what happens when they malfunction. Parody and inversion are two strategies which operate in this way as frame-breaks. The alternation of frame and frame-break (or the construction of an illusion through the imperceptibility of the frame and the shattering of illusion through the constant exposure of the frame) provides the essential deconstructive method of metafiction.

It seems that, according to Goffman, our sense of reality is strong enough to cope with minor frame-breaks, and in fact they reaffirm it, ensuring

> the continuity and viability of the established frame. Indeed the disattend track specifically permits the occurrence of many out-of-frame acts, provided only that they are 'properly' muted, that is, within the disattend capacity of the frame. . . . Thus collusive exchanges between friends at stylish gatherings can be at once a means of breaking frame and a means of staying within it.
>
> (Goffman 1974, p. 382)

This comment is interesting because it offers support for an intuitive sense that although Fielding, Trollope and George Eliot, for example, often 'break the frame' of their novels they are by no means self-conscious novelists in the sense in which the term has been discussed here. Although the intrusive

commentary of nineteenth-century fiction may at times be metalingual (referring to fictional codes themselves), it functions
mainly to aid the readerly concretization of the world of the
book by forming a bridge between the historical and the fictional
worlds. It suggests that the one is merely a continuation of the
other, and it is thus not metafictional.

In *Adam Bede* (1859), for example, George Eliot destroys the
illusion of Hayslope's self-containedness by continually intruding moralistic commentary, interpretation and appeals to the
reader. However, such intrusions do in fact *reinforce* the connection between the real and the fictional world, *reinforce* the
reader's sense that one is a continuation of the other. In
metafictional texts such intrusions *expose* the ontological distinctness of the real and the fictional world, *expose* the literary
conventions that disguise this distinctness. In the chapter entitled 'The Rector', the narrative voice intrudes: 'Let me take
you into their dining room . . . we will enter, very softly . . . the
walls you see, are new. . . . He will perhaps turn round by and
by and in the meantime we can look at that stately old lady' (p.
63). Eliot is here using the convention of the reader's presence
and the author's limitations – a pretence that neither knows
what will happen next – to suggest through the collusive
interchange that both are situated in ontologically undifferenti-
ated worlds. Although this is a frame-break, therefore, it is of the
minor variety which, in Goffman's terms, *reinforces* the illusion.

In order to clarify the implications of the difference between a
minor and a major frame-break, and their respective uses in
realistic and metafictional novels, *Adam Bede* can be compared
with a metafictional novel, set at roughly the same time and in
many ways involving similar moral issues. John Fowles's *The
French Lieutenant's Woman* uses the device of authorial intimacy
ultimately to *destroy* the illusion of reality. Throughout the
fiction, real documents are referred to – as, for example, in the
description of Sarah unpacking at Exeter. The narrator meticulously describes each article that she takes out:

> and then a Toby Jug, not one of those greenish-coloured
> monstrosities of Victorian manufacture, but a delicate little
> thing . . . (certain experts may recognize a Ralph Leigh) . . .

the toby was cracked and was to be recracked in the course of time, as I can testify, having bought it myself a year or two ago for a good deal more than the three pennies Sarah was charged. But unlike her I fell for the Ralph Leigh part of it. She fell for the smile.

(p. 241)

Sarah and the toby jug appear to have the same ontological status as the narrator. This brings the reader up against the paradoxical realization that normally we can read novels only because of our suspension of disbelief. Of course we *know* that what we are reading is not 'real', but we suppress the knowledge in order to increase our enjoyment. We tend to read fiction as if it were history. By actually appearing to treat the fiction as a historical document, Fowles employs the convention against itself. The effect of this, instead of *reinforcing* our sense of a continuous reality, is to split it open, to *expose* the levels of illusion. We are forced to recall that our 'real' world can *never* be the 'real' world of the novel. So the frame-break, while appearing to bridge the gap between fiction and reality, in fact lays it bare.

Throughout *The French Lieutenant's Woman* there is an abundance of frame-breaks more overt than this, particularly where the twentieth-century narrator suddenly appears as a character in the *histoire* as well as in the *discours*. The effect is one which Goffman has again discussed: 'When a character comments on a whole episode of activity in frame terms, he acquires a peculiar reality through the same words by which he undermines the one that was just performed' (Goffman 1974, p. 400). When Fowles discusses the fact that 'these characters I create never existed outside my own mind' (pp. 84–5), the peculiar reality forced upon the reader is that the character who is the apparent teller of the tale is its inventor and not a recorder of events that happened (this becomes the entire theme of Raymond Federman's novel *Double or Nothing*). Fowles goes on to argue, of course, that 'Fiction is woven into all. . . . I find this new reality (or unreality) more valid' (pp. 86–7).

Despite this effect of exposure, however, it can be argued that metafictional novels simultaneously strengthen each reader's sense of an everyday real world while problematizing his or her sense of reality from a conceptual or philosophical point of view. As a consequence of their metafictional undermining of the conventional basis of existence, the reader may revise his or her ideas about the philosophical status of what is assumed to be reality, but he or she will presumably continue to believe and live in a world for the most part constructed out of 'common sense' and routine. What writers like Fowles are hoping is that each reader does this with a new awareness of how the meanings and values of that world have been constructed and how, therefore, they can be challenged or changed. To some extent each metafictional novel is a fictional *Mythologies* which, like Roland Barthes's work, aims to unsettle our convictions about the relative status of 'truth' and 'fiction'. As Goffman argues:

> The study of how to uncover deceptions is also by and large the study of how to build up fabrications . . . one can learn how one's sense of ordinary reality is produced by examining something that is easier to become conscious of, namely, how reality is mimicked and/or how it is faked.
>
> (Goffman 1974, p. 251)

Play, games and metafiction

All art is 'play' in its creation of other symbolic worlds; 'fiction is primarily an elaborate way of pretending, and pretending is a fundamental element of play and games' (Detweiler 1976, p. 51). Without necessarily accepting the Freudian notion that art and literature act as compensatory forms of gratification replacing for an adult the lost childhood world of play and escapism, it can be argued not only that literary fiction is a form of play (if a very sophisticated form) but that play is an important and necessary aspect of human society. It is clear that metafictional writers view play in this light – Ronald Sukenick, for example, in a story entitled 'The Death of the Novel' (1969): 'What we need is not great works but playful ones. . . . A story is a game someone has played so you can play it too' (pp. 56–7) – and it is clear that psychologists like L. S. Vygotsky (1971), Jean Piaget (1951) and Gregory Bateson (1972) share this perception.

However, it is also clear that critics of metafiction either disagree with psychologists' and sociologists' view of play as educative and enlightening or disagree with the notion of art as play. For metafiction sets out to make this explicit: that play is a relatively autonomous activity but has a definite value in the real world. Play is facilitated by rules and roles, and metafiction operates by exploring fictional rules to discover the role of fictions in life. It aims to discover how we each 'play' our own realities.

The metacommentary provided by self-conscious fiction carries the more or less explicit message: 'this is make-believe' or 'this is play'. The most important feature shared by fiction and play is the construction of an alternative reality by manipulating the relation between a set of signs (whether linguistic or non-linguistic) as 'message' and the context or frame of that message. As Bateson argues in *Steps to an Ecology of Mind*, the same behaviour can be 'framed' by a shift in context which then requires very different interpretative procedures. The same set of actions performed in a 'play' context will not denote what they signify in a non-play context. Roland Barthes demonstrates this very entertainingly in his analysis of wrestling in *Mythologies*. The sport is praised for its 'semiotic' as opposed to 'mimetic' construction of meaning, its flaunting of its status as play. The spectators are never deluded into believing that a 'real' fight is taking place; they are kept constantly aware that it is a spectacle:

> only an image is involved in the game, and the spectator does not wish for the actual suffering of the contestant; he only enjoys the perfection of an iconography. It is not true that wrestling is a sadistic spectacle: it is only an intelligible spectacle.
>
> (Barthes 1972b, p. 20)

Literary fiction, as a form of play, shifts signification in the same way. In fact the shift of context is greater because fiction is constructed with language and language is characterized precisely by its detachability from specific context. Language does not have to refer to objects and situations immediately present at the act of utterance; it does not have to be directly indexical. A phrase uttered in a real-life context and referring to objects actually present can be transferred to many different contexts: everyday, literary, journalistic, philosophical, scientific. The actual relationship of the signs within the phrase will remain the same, but, because their relationship to signs outside themselves has shifted, the meaning of the phrase will also shift. Thus the language of fiction may appear to imitate the languages of the everyday world, but its 'meaning' will necessarily be different. However, all play and fiction require 'meta' levels which explain the transition from one context to another and set up a hierarchy of contexts and meanings. In metafiction this level is foregrounded to a considerable extent because the main concern of metafiction is precisely the implications of the shift from the context of 'reality' to that of 'fiction' and the complicated interpenetration of the two.

Bateson saw play as a means of discovering new communicative possibilities, since the 'meta' level necessary for play allows human beings to discover how they can manipulate behaviour and contexts. The subsequent discovery of new methods of communication allows for adaptation, which he sees as ensuring human survival. Fictional play also re-evaluates the traditional procedures of communication and allows release from established patterns. Metafiction explicitly examines the relation of these procedures within the novel to procedures outside it, ensuring the survival through adaptability of the novel itself.

Metafiction draws attention to the process of recontextualization that occurs when language is used aesthetically — when language is, in the sense described above, used 'playfully'. Most psychologists of play emphasize this release from everyday contexts. They argue that 'a certain degree of choice, lack of constraint from conventional ways of handling objects, materials and ideas, is inherent in the concept of play. This is its main connexion with art' (Millar 1968, p. 21). When such a shift of context occurs, though, the more dislocatory it is (say, from the everyday to literary fantasy rather than to literary realism), the more the shift itself acts implicitly as a metacommenting frame. Without *explicit* metacommentary, however, the process of recontextualization is unlikely to be fully understood, and this may result in an unintentional confusion of planes or orders of reality.

This was demonstrated very clearly in fact by Jakobson's work on speech disturbances or aphasia (Jakobson 1956). In what Jakobson referred to as 'similarity disorder', the aphasic person suffers from an incapacity to 'name' objects (an incapacity to manipulate language through the activity of substitution) and a tendency to rely on metonymy. In this disorder, the aphasic cannot use words unless the objects to which the words refer are immediately present. Language thus loses its central characteristic of detachability from context. The more dependent the message on the *immediate* context, therefore, the more likely is the aphasic to understand it. Jakobson suggests that this disorder is 'properly a loss of metalanguage' (ibid., p. 67). Although linguistic messages can operate outside their immediate referential contexts, metalanguage (reference to the codes of language themselves) is needed for this to be successful. The more 'playful' a literary work (the more, for example, it shifts from everyday to alternative-world contexts), the more such metalanguages are needed if the relationship between the 'real' and the 'fictive' world is to be maintained and understood. In metafictional novels it is the nature of this relationship which is the subject of enquiry. Metalingual commentary is thus foregrounded as the *vehicle* of that enquiry.

In some novels, contexts shift so continuously and unsystematically that the metalingual commentary is not adequate to 'place' or to interpret such shifts. The reader is *deliberately* disoriented (as in the novels of William Burroughs, for example). Alternatively, some contemporary novels are constructed with extreme shifts of context or frame (from realism to fantasy, for instance), but without any explanatory metalingual commentary to facilitate the transition from one to the other. The reader is thus neither offered a rational explanation for the shift nor provided with any means of relating one context to another.

Gabriel García Márquez's novel *One Hundred Years of Solitude* (1967) achieves its bizarre effects through this type of shift. Ostensibly realistically portrayed characters suddenly begin to act in fantastic ways. Characters die and come back to life, a man is turned into a snake 'for having disobeyed his parents' (p. 33). Similarly, in Leonard Michaels's 'Mildred' (1964) a tense conversation is interrupted by one of the characters literally starting to eat the womb of one of the others, and finally the narrator starts to eat his face. Michaels gives no indication that this surrealist dislocation may be based on a confusion of the *metaphorical* 'eating one's heart out' (based on context detachability) with its *literal* meaning when returned to context. In other words, he deliberately uses 'similarity disorder' in reverse. The effect in both of these examples is close to that of a schizophrenic construction of reality (as Bateson sees it), where information is not processed, where metalingual insufficiency results in a failure to distinguish between hierarchies of messages and contexts. Here the historical world and the alternative or fantasy world merge. In metafiction they are always held in a state of tension, and the relationship between them – between 'play' and 'reality' – is the main focus of the text.

It is therefore play as a rule-governed activity, one involving 'assimilation of' and 'accommodation to' (Piaget's terms) the structures of the everyday world, as much as play as a form of escapism, of release from 'having to mean', which interests metafictional writers. As Gina Politi has argued:

> There is some truth in the historical fact that whenever man has to be defined as man equals child, the edenic period whereby he can live without structures is short-lived and another game is invented which brings in the law-maker who declares what games are and what they are not.
>
> (Politi 1976, p. 60)

Golding's *Lord of the Flies* (1954) achieved the success it did because of its accurate perception of this point.

Another fictional response to the sense of oppression by the endless systems and structures of present-day society – with its technologies, bureaucracies, ideologies, institutions and traditions – is the construction of a play world which consists of similar endless systems and structures. Thomas Pynchon and Joseph McElroy both construct novels whose vast proliferation of counter-systems and counter-games suggests one way of eluding the apparent predetermination of the structures of the everyday world. Pynchon's *Gravity's Rainbow* and McElroy's *Lookout Cartridge* (1974) function through informational overload and apparent overdetermination. However, the systems and structures presented to the reader never add up to a body of meaning or an interpretation. Documentation, obsessional systems, the languages of commerce, of the legal system, of popular culture, of advertising: hundreds of systems compete with each other, collectively resisting assimilation to any one received paradigm and thus the normal channels of data-processing.

In McElroy's *A Smuggler's Bible* (1966) the central motif of smuggling, of counterfeiting, of forging, of deceiving, set against the 'absolute truth', the concordance of origins and endings of the Bible, is explored as much through what the language *is* as what it *says*. The central character David Brooke, like Borges' mnemonist, suffers from total recall of information and breaks down. The novel also breaks down. Neither Brooke nor the novel can absorb and organize the numerous and contradictory codes and registers of language with which they are both confronted and constructed. Mythical, biblical, numerical, geographical, physical and metaphysical explanations break down into a total overdetermination of meaning, which therefore becomes meaningless.

The image of the smuggler's bible is in fact just one of the many examples in recent literature of versions of the 'black box', contemporary culture's answer to the Grail. The image appears explicitly in another story concerned with human attempts to resist technological and social determinism: Barthelme's 'The Explanation', in the collection entitled *City Life* (1970). The story is a parody of an interview between an anonymous Q and A about the identity and meaning of a black box which is typographically reproduced at the beginning of the story. At one level the story is simply and directly metafictional: it is 'about' the non-interpretability of itself:

Q: It has beauties
A: The machine
Q: Yes. We construct these machines not because we confidently expect them to do what they are designed to do – change the government in this instance – but because we

intuit a machine out there, glowing like a shopping centre.

(p. 72)

Halfway through, Q introduces a series of 'error messages', corrections by a computer of uninterpretable programs, which in this instance all refer to the story itself, in a 'computerized' literary-critical discourse:

> undefined variable . . . improper sequence of operators . . . improper use of hierarchy . . . missing operator . . . mixed mode, that one's particularly grave . . . argument of a function is fixed-point . . . improper character in constant . . . invalid character transmitted in sub-program statement, that's a bitch . . . no END statement

(p. 73)

Later, Q tells the reader: 'The issues are not real in the sense that they are touchable.' A (the reader substitute within the story), however, still manages to process the message, sees in the black box a face, an extraordinarily handsome girl stripping, a river, a chair, a human narrative, or at least the raw materials of one. Barthelme's story dramatizes the human propensity to construct its own systems and interpretations in order to resist technological determinism and dehumanization. If the machine operates in terms of its own cybernetic game theory, Barthelme shows that his fiction can operate through simply recontextualizing its messages within his own 'play' world.

Such fiction, however, moves towards a form of play which one theorist has termed the 'illinx': an entropic, self-annihilating form which represents an attempt to 'momentarily destroy the stability of perceptions and inflict a kind of voluptuous panic upon an otherwise lucid mind . . . a kind of seizure or shock which destroys reality with sovereign brusqueness' (Caillois 1962, p. 25). Fictions of aleation or randomness can be placed in this category. Metafiction functions through the problematization rather than the destruction of the concept of 'reality'. It depends on the regular construction and subversion of rules and systems. Such novels usually set up an internally consistent 'play' world which ensures the reader's absorption, and then lays bare its rules in order to investigate the relation of 'fiction' to 'reality', the concept of 'pretence'.

Two theories of play will briefly be considered here: that of Johan Huizinga in *Homo Ludens: A Study of the Play Element in Culture* (1949) and that of Roger Caillois in *Man, Play and Games* (1962). Huizinga defines play as a free activity which 'transpires in an explicitly circumscribed time and space, is carried out in an orderly fashion according to given rules and gives rise to group relations which often surround themselves with mystery or emphasize through disguises their difference from the ordinary world' (Huizinga 1949, pp. 34–5). This accords with the notion of 'play' implicit in most metafictional novels.

There is a central contradiction in both Huizinga's and Caillois's definition of play, however, which is precisely where metafictional interest is focused. They appear to argue that the main significance of play is its civilizing influence, but Huizinga explicitly states at one point that he sees civilization becoming less and less playful. Yet elsewhere he argues that he sees 'man' as becoming more and more civilized. The way out of this problem (and the perspective asserted by most metafictional writing) is implicit in the second part of Caillois's book where he argues that it is precisely an awareness of play *as* play which constitutes the civilizing, as opposed to the brutally instinctual, possibilities of play. The positive emphasis thus shifts to the laying bare of the rules of the game. 'Illinx' becomes associated with attempts at pure mimesis and is seen to result in alienation. The player loses him or herself in a fantasy world and actually becomes the role being played (a favourite metafictional theme – as, for example, in Muriel Spark's *The Public Image* (1968)) or attempts to impose it on others as 'reality'. In literature, then, realism, more than aleatory art, becomes the mode most threatening to full civilization, and metafiction becomes the mode most conducive to it!

The current 'playfulness' within the novel is certainly not confined merely to literary form but is part of a broader development in culture which is registered acutely in all postmodernist art. As Michael Beaujour suggests:

The desire to play a game in reverse usually arises when the straight way of playing has become a bore . . . the rules of the game, which although arbitrary, had somehow become 'natural' to the players, now seem artificial, tyrannical and dead: the system does not allow for sufficient player freedom within it and must be discarded. Although only a system can replace a system, the interregnum may be experienced as total freedom. In fact, it is but the moment of a new deal.

(Beaujour 1968, p. 60)

Freedom is the moment when the game or the genre is being discarded, but the rules of the new one are not yet defined and are therefore experienced as the 'waning of former rules' (ibid.). Metafiction is in the position of examining the old rules in order to discover new possibilities of the game. In its awareness of the serious possibility of play, it in fact echoes some of the major concerns of twentieth-century thought: Piaget's work on the educational value of play; Wittgenstein's view of language as a set of games; the existential notion of reality as a game of being; the possibility of the endless play of language through the release of the signifier in post-structuralist theory such as that of Lacan or Derrida and, of course, the proliferation of popular psychology books such as Eric Berne's *Games People Play*. Even in the commercial world, game theory is an increasingly important aspect of systems analysis. A new emphasis on the importance of discovering fresh combinations in probability and risk is shown in the application of game theory, for example, to economic or political problems.

Some metafictional novelists make the reader explicitly aware of his or her role as player. The reader of *The French Lieutenant's Woman*, having to choose an ending, becomes a player in the game, one very much modelled on the Heideggerian game of being. In the title story of B. S. Johnson's *Aren't You Rather Young to be Writing Your Memoirs* (1973), an adventure story in which nothing happens, the reader is told to 'provide your own surmises or even your own ending, as you are inclined' (p. 41). Barthelme and Federman present the reader with acrostics, puzzles to be solved, and black boxes or blank pages to interpret, according to the reader's own fictional predilections. Calvino's novel, *If on a Winter's Night a Traveller*, addresses the reader in the second person and explicitly discusses the supremacy of his or her activity in realizing the text imaginatively.

The 'Dear Reader' is no longer quite so passive and becomes in effect an acknowledged fully active player in a new conception of literature as a collective creation rather than a monologic and authoritative version of history.

All metafiction 'plays' with the form of the novel, but not all playfulness in fiction is of the metafictional variety. Metafiction very deliberately undermines a system, unlike, say, aleatory or Dadaist art which attempts to embrace randomness or 'illinx'. In a novel like Brautigan's *Trout Fishing in America*, there is playfulness but none of the systematic flaunting characteristic of metafiction. (The effect is perhaps closer to that of Márquez's fictions, where fantastic events and situations are integrated into a basically realistic context with no narratorial hint of their impossibility or absurdity.) Only a common deployment of the title links the separate sections of the novel. It is metafictional only to the extent that it foregrounds the arbitrary relationship between words and things and lays bare the construction of meaning through metaphorical substitution. For the most part, it is fabulatory because the reader is never required systematically to connect the artifice of the narrative with the problematic 'real' world, or to explore the mode of fictional presentation.

Another sort of fiction is that built around the idea or rules of an actual game, as in Coover's 'Panel Game' (1971) or *The Universal Baseball Association, Inc.* (1968) and Nabokov's *The Defence* (1964). The latter, for example, is close to metafiction in that the game of chess, traditionally a metaphor for life, is used here as a metaphor for the strategies of art. Luzhin is one of Nabokov's familiar artist *manqué* figures, playing blind games of chess in order to achieve abstract perfection until the 'consecutive repetition of a familiar pattern' (p. 168) becomes an invincible opponent taking over his life. In a state of paranoia similar to Woolf's Septimus Smith, he throws himself out of the window and dies in what his chess-obsessed mind has taken to be a real-life game. The novel suggests that each person is to some extent the victim of his or her own games with reality, but that the mistake is to search for a perfect form of order.

The 'problem of the equality of appearance and numbers' (*Pricksongs and Descants*, p. 8) – that is, of play with combination and permutation – is a favourite device in metafiction. Writers employing such techniques, through a heightened sense of the randomness of the world, have come to see its configuration, in whatever mathematical or other combination they choose, as just as correspondent with reality as the paradigms of realism. Italo Calvino suggests that the combinative impulse has been basic to literature from the beginning; that in ancient times 'the storyteller would delve into the natural resources of his own stock of words. He did this by combinations and permutations of all the characters, activities and tangible objects which could be invoked in the repertoire of actions' (Calvino 1970, p. 93). He suggests that this forms a kind of generative grammar of narrative which makes renewal possible. Combinative play in metafiction is concerned with the self-consciously performed reintroduction into the literary system of previously outworn modes and the exposure of present exhausted forms often unrecognized as such. Further, the element of chance in combination may throw up a whole new possibility which rational exploration might not have discovered.

Samuel Beckett begins with the perception that habit and routine form the substructure of most individual existences. He therefore uses both as the starting point for his fiction and pushes them to a logical extreme which reveals not only their *absurdity* but also their *necessity* in a world that has no innate structure of its own. Malone tells himself stories that are made to correspond, through his own conceptualizations, with the apparent structure of his life, which itself turns out to be only the story he narrates. He provides variety in this life by means of the slightly shifting repetitions that he consciously forces upon the narrative process. *Malone Dies* (1951) has to be understood in these terms, for the patterns Malone sets up seem to bear not even an analogous relationship to the meaning of the world outside him.

In *Watt* (1953) the protagonist totally replaces the world with his verbal constructs when he realizes the impossibility of transcribing it. In attempting to grasp the meaning of phenomena, he enumerates every possible combination and permutation he can think of for each set of circumstances, in an attempt to construct a system which will offer him a stable identity. However, as Mr Nixon tells Mr Hackett, 'I tell you nothing is known. Nothing' (p. 20). The human mind is a fallible instrument of measurement and the external world a chaos. Knowledge derived from human calculation or generalization can only demonstrate the epistemological distance between consciousness and objective reality, however exhaustive the account. The Lynch family, attempting to total one thousand years of age between them, have their calculations completely undermined by the textual superiority of the footnote informing the reader: 'The figures given here are incorrect. The consequent calculations are . . . doubly erroneous' (p. 101). Even if the figures were not in some epistemological doubt, the reader's attention has anyway been called to the ontological status of the fictional text. Watt's life is full of similarly fruitless calculations, like the half-page of combinations of 'man' and 'woman' in the attempt to settle the question of whether Mrs Gorman is a 'Man's woman' and whether she and Watt will therefore suit each other. The passage begins with an oscillation between polarities – of gender, of rhymes (the arbitrary sound-relations in language such as 'Watt' and 'not'), of terms like 'call' and 'countercall' – but this simple binary opposition is abandoned, to end with: 'that meant nothing' (p. 141) (not even the binary opposition of all *or* nothing but the identity of all *with* nothing).

The problem is that to cover the infinite number of possible situations that can arise from a finite number of experiences would involve the use of infinite numbers of words and repetitions. Beckett's attempt to show this makes the text become rather like an official form which asks one to delete the irrelevant information. The contradiction between, on the one hand, an abstract methodology which constructs a 'system' and, on the other, the apparent concrete illogical 'reality' of experience in the world (which Realism chooses to treat as one and the same) is, in fact, irreconcilable. So Watt constructs his own system of 'Kriks' and 'Kraks'. Instead of trying to force correspondence between his system and the world, he simply ignores the world.

Many of Beckett's characters spend their fictional lives in various forms of serious play, attempting to come to terms with this problem. Combination is foregrounded even on a stylistic level, as in *Waiting for Godot* (1956): 'Let us not then speak ill of our generation. . . . Let us not speak well of it either. . . . Let us not speak of it at all. . . . It is true the population has increased' (p. 33). This spiralling sentence structure is very common in much of his work. So is the use of contradiction, as in the end of 'Dante and the Lobster' (*More Pricks than Kicks*, 1934): 'Well, thought Belacqua, it's a quick death, God help us all. It is not' (p. 19), which functions in a way and with effects similar to the footnote in *Watt*.

In *Imagination Dead Imagine* (1965) the second sentence, 'Islands, waters, azure, verdure, one glimpse and vanished, endlessly omit', suggests that poetic descriptions are no longer valid, and substitutes the mathematical: 'Diameter three feet, three feet from ground. . . . Two diameters at right angles AB CD divide the white ground into two semicircles ACB BDA.' The human subject is suddenly inserted into the geometry problem – 'the head against the wall at B, the arse against the wall at A, the knees against the wall between B and C' – and the text breaks down into a series of oppositions: white/black, human/mathematical, light/dark, heat/ice, in a sequence again of colliding combinations which reduce this world to variations on the alignments of ABCD (pp. 7–14).

Calvino's fiction also uses these strategies of combination. In *The Castle of Crossed Destinies* (1969) a footnote tells the reader that the 'author' (who is effectively made redundant by the information) generated the text in the manner reproduced in fact by the narrative situation: a group of characters who are mute tell their stories by selecting and combining the images from a pack of tarot cards. These combinations and selections, drawing from a total system of literature (a *langue*), produce individual utterances (*paroles*) or stories which have meaning only through their differential relation with implied archetypal stories recurring throughout: *Oedipus*, the Grail legend, *Lear*, *Hamlet*, *Macbeth*. The contemporary 'author', now the contemporary categorizer, is himself produced through the textual combinations. He believes that to write a 'great work' of literature simply involves the provision of a reference catalogue of existing 'great works', an ultimate intertextual key. The possibilities of 'literature as system' begin to obsess him, until he realizes: 'It was absurd to waste any more time on an operation whose implicit possibilities I had by now explored completely, an operation that made sense only as theoretical hypothesis' (p. 120).

Calvino's *If on a Winter's Night a Traveller* discovers a more effective way out of this endlessly permutating system: the use of overtly metafictional, and in particular parodistic, devices. The novel opens with a direct address to the reader in the situation of reading, and a metalingual discourse upon the construction of the plot and the relation of *histoire* to *discours*. This confuses the ontological levels of the text with descriptions like: 'The novel begins in a railway station . . . a cloud of smoke hides the first part of the paragraph' (p. 8). Here the situation of *narration* is confused with the situation of the *histoire*, reminding the reader that descriptions in novels are always creations of that which is to be described: that the language in this sense refers ultimately to itself. Throughout we are reminded of the status of the book as an *artefact* through references to missing pages, pages stuck together, disordered pages. We are reminded also of its *intertextual* existence through the fragments of novels, stories and narratives embedded within the outer frame. (Again this is a very common metafictional device, used extensively, for example, by Flann O'Brien, B. S. Johnson, John Irving and Donald Barthelme.) Both Beckett and Calvino metafictionally 'play' with possibilities of combination, but through techniques like irony provide themselves with escape routes from the endless permutations of systems which might continually change their surface forms but which retain their inherent structures. Other novelists may choose to impose extreme formal constraints on themselves, which, in their arbitrariness, metafictionally reflect back on the conventional contracts which legitimize 'meaning'. Two examples of this literary production in a very closed field are Walter Abish's *Alphabetical Africa* (1974) and Gilbert Sorrentino's *Splendide-Hotel* (1973).

Alphabetical Africa works on the principle that every sentence in the first chapter is composed only of words beginning with 'A'. Chapter 2 adds 'B' words, and so on. The linguistic structure dictates both formal effects and meaning. The narrator, for example, cannot be introduced as a person until 'I'. He literally awaits creation through language. Alliteration cannot function because, instead of being a technique of linguistic deviance and thus foregrounded, it is the stylistic norm until well into the novel. Even the story and the development of the plot are determined by what can be constructed out of the available linguistic elements. At 'M', therefore, a murder can occur which could change the whole course of the action. At 'O' the reader is told: 'One is always either moving forwards or backwards, one is always driven by insane but meticulously considered needs.' Thus even the historic 'one', the non-person existing outside the discourse, is ultimately constructed through it (explicitly, therefore, through an arbitrary order and set of distinctions).

A similar example of what Abish has referred to as language as a 'field of action' is Sorrentino's *Splendide-Hotel*. Here, however, the letters of the alphabet merely serve to trigger off verbal musings. The Splendide-Hotel, though never defined, is clearly the verbal imagination itself, seen as intrinsically playful rather than intrinsically aesthetic. The narrator intrudes with the information that 'I insist I do not speak of this game as art, yet it is close to art in that it is so narrowly itself: it does not stand for anything else' (p. 14). He thus offers a view of literature similar to that formulated by Roman Jakobson: the view that literature is a message for its own sake, or a message about itself (Jakobson 1960). However, both Abish and Sorrentino, in their self-contained linguistic play, tend to point the direction from metafiction to a 'literature of silence', or a pure formalism, a literature solely concerned with its own linguistic processes.

The linguistic universe: reality as construct

Frame analysis and play theory are areas of contemporary social investigation which illumine the practice of metafiction and show the sensitivity of its reponse to cultural change. They are each, however, aspects of a broader shift in thought and practice whereby reality has increasingly come to be seen as a construct. Hegel, in fact, suggested that history be contemplated as a work of art, for in retrospect it 'reads' like a novel: its end is known. Metafiction suggests not only that writing history is a fictional act, ranging events conceptually through language to form a world-model, but that history itself is invested, like fiction, with interrelating plots which appear to interact independently of human design.

This is the theme of Malcolm Bradbury's *The History Man* (1975). Like much British self-conscious fiction, however, the novel manages to suggest the fictionality of 'reality' without entirely abandoning realism. The only *blatantly* metafictional moment is when an academic novelist, clearly recognizable as a surrogate for Bradbury himself, scurries across the corridor of Watermouth University where the novel is set. (He is, interestingly, presented as a very minor and ineffectual character.) A close analysis of *The History Man*, though, reveals an intense preoccupation, formally as well as thematically, with the notion of history as fiction. Even the opening paragraph is less a piece of realistic prose than a *parody* of realism. The continual use of deliberately well-worn phrases about the Kirks (Howard's 'two well-known and disturbing books'; p. 3); the antithetical structures and parallelisms ('You buy the drinks, I'll buy the food'; p. 8); the juxtaposition of normally unrelated items such as 'a new kind of Viennese coffee cake to eat and a petition to sign' (p. 3): these function not only to parody the Kirks' lifestyle but to foreground the ways in which that lifestyle is also a consequence of Bradbury's obtrusive *linguistic* style.

The Kirks are explicitly 'types' who exist in the service of plot: the plot of history/fiction which envelops the plotter Howard through the superior shaping powers of the novelist himself. He, allowing Howard the delusion of freedom, reminds the reader of his ultimate control through the ironic repetition of events at the end. The significance of these events Howard, of course, fails to grasp, trapped as he is both in his own 'lifestyle' and in Bradbury's 'fictional style'. Howard acts as though he were the embodiment of history and thus in control of both his own and others' destinies. Although 'the days may lie contingently ahead of them . . . the Kirks always have a plot of many events' (p. 52). Howard confuses his own plots, however, with those of history – here constructed through language by Bradbury himself. It is Miss Callendar (whose name suggests time as contingency, as escape from plot) who points out the multiple possibilities of interpretation, the numerous plots that can be drawn out of, or imposed on, any historical or fictional situation. It is she who exposes Howard's plot as 'a piece of late nineteenth-century realism' (p. 209).

The notion of the fictionality of the plots of history is textually reinforced through a variety of techniques. The dialogue, for example, is submerged in the main narrative to suggest the ways in which our individual interpretations are always parts of larger ones. This foregrounds the provisional status within the overall *discours* of *any* character's or narrator's speech act. The reader is taken into the dynamic present tense of Howard's plots, yet reminded of Freud's law of displacement – that it is impossible to see the world other than as we wish it to be – by the ostentatious entries of the greater plot-maker, the novelist, into the text. He functions to set fictional desire against fictional reality and to show how one is translated into the other.

To some extent the idea that life involves the construction of plots has always been a preoccupation of the novel. Richard Poirier, in fact, has suggested that Americans have always treated reality as their own construction; they have always realized that 'through language it is possible to create environments radically different from those supported by political and social systems' (Poirier 1967, p. 16). Thus the notion of history as either a rather badly made plot or a fiendish conspiracy is more deeply rooted in the American than in the British novel.

A comparison of the exploration of plots in John Barth's *The Sot-Weed Factor* (1960) with that undertaken by Bradbury in *The History Man* illustrates very well such differences between these two fictional traditions. The characters in both novels self-consciously participate in plots, whether of their own or others' making. In Barth's novel, however, *all* the characters are self-consciously plotters. Ebenezer argues that what the cosmos lacks human beings must supply themselves, and Burlingame gives philosophic respectability to the notion of plotting, while using it like Howard to gain personal advantages. However, in this world, because the plots are so much more anonymous, proliferating and uncontrollable, the characters' behaviour appears far more desperate and absurd than Howard's self-assured exploitation of Marx, Freud, Hegel and undergraduate innocence. Even Barth's demonstration of his authorial control

through the overplot of the mythic quest is continually and
ironically undercut to give the sense, as Burlingame expresses
it, that 'the very universe is nought but change and motion' (p.
137).

The consequence of this, though, is that, in attempting to
embrace all, his characters embrace nothing but the 'baroque
exhaustion of the frightening guises of reality' (Barth 1967, p.
81). In the novel as a whole, moreover, the metafictional bones
are often left obtruding from a very thin human covering. The
reader is presented, in fact, with a fictional world in many ways
akin to Borges' Tlön, where history lessons teach that 'already a
fictitious past occupies in our memories the place of another, a
past of which we know nothing with certainty – not even that it
is false' (*Labyrinths*, pp. 42–3). In *The History Man* the stable
ironic voice of the author ensures that the reader can observe
and evaluate Howard's version of the past and his imposition of
various images and plots upon the present. But in *The Sot-Weed
Factor* there is no such area of narrative stability. Plot is all.

The concept of reality as a fiction has been theoretically
formulated within many disciplines and from many political
and philosophical positions. One of the clearest *sociological*
expositions is in Peter L. Berger and Thomas Luckmann's
book, *The Social Construction of Reality* (1971). They set out to
show that 'reality' is not something that is simply given. 'Reality' is manufactured. It is produced by the interrelationship of
apparently 'objective facticities' in the world with social convention and personal or interpersonal vision. These social forms
operate within particular historical structures of power and
frameworks of knowledge. Continual shifts in the structures of
knowledge and power produce continual resyntheses of the
reality model. Contemporary reality, in particular, is continually
being reappraised and resynthesized. It is no longer experienced as an ordered and fixed hierarchy, but as a web of
interrelating, multiple realities.

Moving *through* this reality involves moving from one 'reality'
to another. Most of the time, however, we are not conscious of
these shifts. Habit, instrumented through social institutions
and conventions, normally disguises movement between levels,
and confers an apparent homogeneity upon social experience. It

is only when a convention is exposed as such that the lacunae between levels are also exposed.

Berger and Luckmann suggest that convention and habit are necessary because human beings need to have their choices narrowed for significant action to take place. Habit ensures that patterns can be repeated in such a way that the meaning of an action is not retained at the level of consciousness. If this were not so, the action could not be effortlessly performed. (This is also, of course, the basis for realistic fiction. When the conventions regarding fictive time, for example, are undermined in *Tristram Shandy*, the novel never gets under way as an *histoire* but functions only as a self-regarding *discours* which never quite manages to get the story told.) Habitualization provides for direction and specialization, by freeing our energies for more productive ends. It opens up a 'foreground for deliberation and innovation' (Berger and Luckmann 1971, p. 71). Conventions can, however, become oppressive and rigidified, completely naturalized. At this point they need to be re-examined, both in life and in fiction.

Everyday reality is, however, for Berger and Luckmann, 'reality *par excellence*'. It imposes itself massively on consciousness so that, although we may doubt its reality, 'I am obliged to suspend this doubt as I routinely exist in everyday life' (ibid., pp. 35–7). Problems that interrupt this flow are seen to be translated into its terms and assimilated: 'Consciousness always returns to the paramount reality as from an excursion' (ibid., p. 58). According to this view, the 'meta' levels of fictional and social discourse might shift our notion of reality slightly but can never totally undermine it.

Berger and Luckmann argue further, however, that language is the main instrument for maintaining this everyday reality: 'Everyday life is above all, life with and by means of the language I share with my fellow men [*sic!*] (ibid., pp. 39–40). Thus texts which move towards a breakdown of the language system, presenting reality as a set of equally non-privileged competing discourses, *can* be seen as resisting assimilation into the terms of the everyday. They attempt, in fact, radically to unsettle our notion of the 'real'. (Doris Lessing's protagonist Anna, for example, in *The Golden Notebook*, loses her precarious hold on this 'everyday life' when she feels 'at a pitch where words mean nothing' (p. 462), because in this novel 'reality *par excellence*' is represented by the misrepresentational, inauthentic language of 'Free Women' which freezes the everyday – 'British life at its roots' – into a mocking parody of itself.)

What has to be acknowledged is that there are two poles of metafiction: one that finally accepts a substantial real world whose significance is not entirely composed of relationships within language; and one that suggests there can never be an escape from the prisonhouse of language and either delights or despairs in this. The first sort employs *structural* undermining of convention, or parody, using a specific previous text or system for its base (novelists like Fowles, Spark, Vonnegut, Lessing) because language is so pre-eminently the instrument which maintains the everyday. The second is represented by those writers who conduct their fictional experiments even at the level of the *sign* (like Barthelme, Brautigan, Ishmael Reed, Joyce's *Finnegans Wake*) and therefore fundamentally disturb the 'every-day'.

Berger and Luckmann do not, in fact, give enough attention to the centrality of language in constructing everyday reality. It is this exposure of 'reality' in terms of 'textuality', for example, which has provided the main critique of realism. As Barthes argued:

> These facts of language were not perceptible so long as literature pretended to be a transparent expression of either objective calendar time or of psychological subjectivity . . . as long as literature maintained a totalitarian ideology of the referent, or more commonly speaking, as long as literature was 'realistic'.
>
> (Barthes 1972c, p. 138)

By 'these facts', of course, he means the extent to which language *constructs* rather than merely *reflects* everyday life: the extent to which meaning resides in the relations between signs *within* a literary fictional text, rather than in their reference to objects *outside* that text.

Metafictional texts often take as a theme the frustration caused by attempting to relate their linguistic condition to the world outside. Coover's 'Panel Game' (1969) parodies the attempt to find an all-encompassing truth in language, by showing the narrator caught up in a maze of the myriad possibilities of meaning, of *paroles* with no discoverable *langues*, while all the possible functions of language – emotive, referenial, poetic, conative, phatic and, finally, metalingual – whirl around him:

> So think. Stickleback. Freshwaterfish. Freshwaterfish: green seaman. Seaman: semen. Yes, but green: raw? spoiled? vigorous? Stickle: stubble. Or maybe scruple. Back: Bach: Bacchus: bachate: berry. Rawberry? Strawberry.
>
> (*Pricksongs and Descants*, p. 63)

Through the emphasis on the arbitrary associations of sound, rhyme and image, attention is drawn to the *formal* organization of words in literature and away from their *referential* potential. The passage could almost be a deliberate flaunting of Jakobson's notion of literary form (for a full discussion of this, see Lodge 1977a). Jakobson argues that the poetic function of language manifests itself by projecting the paradigmatic or metaphorical dimension of language (the vertical dimension which functions through substitution) on to the syntagmatic or metonymic plane (the horizontal dimension which works through combination). In this passage, the speaker is wholly at the mercy of these internal operations of language, condemned to the substitution of one arbitrary phoneme for another: 'Stickleback. Freshwaterfish [metonymic] Freshwaterfish: green seaman [metonymic/metaphoric] seaman: semen [metaphoric] . . .'

The notion of reality as a construct, explored through textual self-reference, is now firmly embedded in the contemporary novel, even in those novels that appear to eschew radically experimental forms or techniques. Muriel Spark's work is a good example of this development, for she uses textual strategies of self-reference, yet still maintains a strong 'story' line. This alerts the reader to the condition of the text, to its state of 'absence', just as much as a novel by Sorrentino or Sarraute or any other more obviously post-modernist writer whose embodiment of the paradoxes of fictionality necessitates the total rejection of traditional concepts of plot and character.

In Spark's first novel *The Comforters* (1957) the character Mrs Hogg (the name itself undermines the tendency of realistic fiction to assign apparently 'arbitrary' non-descriptive names to characters) forces her overwhelming physical and mental presence upon the other characters and upon the reader. The novel, however, goes on to delight in demonstrating the impossibility of this presence. Her physical grossness appears to be metaphorically (and conventionally realistically) related to her inner moral condition. She appears, in this sense, to be a full presence. Yet, shortly after one of the characters utters the familiar metaphorical cliché that Mrs Hogg appears to be 'not all there', the narrator informs us that 'as soon as Mrs Hogg stepped into her room, she disappeared, she simply disappeared. She had no private life whatsoever, God knows where she went in her privacy' (p. 154). Mrs Hogg's absence becomes as troublesome and problematical as her huge and physically grotesque presence. When Caroline (the central character who becomes aware that her life is writing itself into a novel) opens the door to Mrs Hogg's knock, she at first receives the impression that 'nobody was there', and afterwards Mrs Hogg is described as 'pathetic and lumpy as a public response' (p. 182).

The incongruous tagging of an adjective normally tied to objects as physically palpable as Mrs Hogg to something as intangible as a 'public response' brings into focus the relationship between her spiritual and physical reality. She is simultaneously, massively, physically *present* and totally, spiritually *absent*. Through an ostensibly whimsical trick, Spark raises a *moral* point about the ethics of those who 'stand for' goodness and righteousness and ultimately become slaves to the public image of their cause. Such people, like Hogg with her fanatical moral intrusiveness, thereby corrupt the inner worth of their causes. Beyond this, however, Spark also makes an *ontological* point concerning the status of fictional objects. Georgiana Hogg is a public figure in all senses of the word because she is contained by, and exists through, the public medium of language. Thus, having been designated a minor role in the plot, when not essential to its unfolding, she does not exist. The moral and existential points are both made through the meta-fictional exposure.

The device is used throughout Spark's work, but always with some realistic motivation. Characters are never presented merely as words on the page. Lise, in *The Driver's Seat* (1970), sustains the plot momentum by her desperate search for a man to murder her. She does not know the man but can confidently identify him: 'not really a presence, the lack of an absence' (p. 71) – a remark which could stand, of course, as a definition of any character in fiction. Humphrey Place in *The Ballad of Peckham Rye* (1960) is given a similar point of view when he replies to the chameleon-like Dougal's suggestion that he take time off: 'No I don't agree to that . . . absenteeism is downright immoral' (p. 49); and he later affirms, 'once you start absenting yourself you lose your self-respect' (p. 87).

Characters are absent because they are linguistic signs, and because they are morally deficient. In the earlier novels the connection between the aesthetic and the moral interpretation of the word 'absenteeism' is based on the perceived connection between inventing a character in fiction and fictionalizing in life in order to escape moral responsibility and to glorify the self. In *The Comforters* this self is a moral reformer, Mrs Hogg. The self might be a great pedagogue and leader, Jean Brodie, or a great aesthete ('each new death gave him something fresh to feel'), Percy Mannering (*Memento Mori* (1959), p. 22). The self can even be a mask, an actress, 'something between Jane Eyre, a heroine of D. H. Lawrence and the governess in *The Turn of the Screw*' – Annabel in *The Public Image* (p. 20). In the later novels, *Not to Disturb* (1971) or *The Abbess of Crewe* (1974), aesthetic and moral issues become interchangeable, so the Abbess does not long for beatification but declares at the end of the novel: 'I am become an object of art' (p. 125).

Characters in fiction are, of course, literally signs on a page before they are anything else. The implications of this provide a fairly simple creative starting point for much metafictional play. Is a character more than a word or a set of words? B. S. Johnson, for example, is clearly drawn towards a traditional liberal-humanist treatment of his characters and yet displays the conviction that they exist merely as the words he chooses to put on the page. In *Christie Malry's Own Double Entry* (1973) Johnson continually intrudes into the text to remind the reader that Christie is whatever fortuitous collection of words happened to enter his head during composition. Yet, at his death-bed scene, the necessary human awfulness of the situation forces Johnson to abandon his focus on *verbal* interaction and to shift to apparent *interpersonal* relationship. The author visits Christie in hospital, 'and the nurses suggested I leave, not knowing who I was, that he could not die without me' (p. 180). The self-conscious literary irony is clearly secondary to the pathos and absurdity of the represented human situation.

Johnson uneasily accommodates a notion of 'absence', an awareness of the linguistic construction of the reality of the text, within a broadly based realistic framework. He never abandons realism in the manner of the *nouveau roman*, of American writers such as Barthelme or Brautigan, or even of such British fiction as that of Christine Brooke-Rose and Ann Quin or Brigid Brophy's *In Transit* (1969). In many of these writers' novels the sign as sign to a large extent overtly replaces any imaginary referent such as realism might offer. To be aware of the sign is thus to be aware of the absence of that to which it apparently refers and the presence only of relationships with other signs within the text. The novel becomes primarily a world of words, self-consciously a replacement for, rather than an appurtenance of, the everyday world.

Again, although this awareness of the problems of representation is far from new, it has clearly come to dominate contemporary critical theory, and increasingly fiction itself. It is true to say, though, that in most British writing the problem tends to be explored thematically, or through macro-structures like plot and narrative voice. The problem of 'absence' is here an extension of the notion that a fictional world is created by a real author through a series of choices about the deployment of linguistic units, but nevertheless in some sense constitutes a version of the everyday world. The sign as sign is still, to a large extent, self-effacing in such fiction.

Ernst Cassirer made the point that signs and symbols have to annul presence to arrive at representation. An existing object is made knowable only through a symbol – by being translated into something it is not. The given can thus be known only through the non-given (the symbol), without which we would have no access to empirical reality. As Cassirer puts it: 'Without the relations of unity and otherness, of similarity and dissimilarity, of identity and difference, the work of intuition can acquire no fixed form' (quoted in Iser 1975, p. 17). In other words, it is *because* symbols are not reality and do not embody any of the actual properties of the world that they allow us to perceive this world, and ultimately to construct it for ourselves and be constructed within it. Writing necessitates 'absence', and to this extent metafictional writers like Muriel Spark can be seen fictionally to embody this ultimately 'commonsense', rather than 'radical' position.

John Fowles explores the concept from a similar, finally realistically motivated position in his story 'The Enigma' (1969). The exploration is provided with a foundation in psychological realism through the disappearance of the establishment figure of John Marcus Fielding. The missing-person motif is, of course, one of the best-established conventions of that supremely rational genre, the detective story. Here, as in Spark's novels, however, it is used in contravention. Through the metafictional play with definitions of fictional character, the motif is used to suggest possibilities which totally confound rational solution.

Fielding, as his son's ex-girlfriend suggests, seems to have disappeared because he felt himself, in Pirandellian fashion, to have been in the wrong story: 'There was an author in his life. In a way not a man. A system, a view of things? Something that had written him. Had really made him just a character in a book' (*The Ebony Tower*, p. 237). Again, thematic concerns are picked up at a level of formal self-reflexivity. Fielding, she suggests, feels himself to lack identity. He is no 'different' from the stereotype of the upper-class member of the British establishment, and the only way of escaping his 'typicality' is to disappear: from the story, and from the 'typicality', the print, of the story itself. Once he has become a mystery, he exists as an individual, for 'Nothing lasts like a mystery. On condition that it stays that way. If he's traced, found, then it all crumbles again. He's back in a story, being written. A nervous breakdown. A nutcase. Whatever' (p. 239). Thus Fielding, through a recognition or 'laying bare' of his absence, becomes a real presence for the first time to the other characters in the story. But Fowles as author can also remind the reader that Fielding exists only if he cannot be 'traced', only if he is more than a literary-fictional 'character'. He never allows Fielding to rewrite his *own* story, only to change its interpretation through his disappearance. In fact, the effect of reading the hypothetical version of this disappearance is another reminder that the character Fielding is at the disposition of the author Fowles. The theory of his disappearance, which might be satisfactory 'in reality', appears to the reader as part of a text which he or she knows, and is then forced to admit, is *not* real. Attention is thus shifted away from the solution of the mystery towards an examination of the conventions governing the presentation of enigma in fiction.

The fiction of Johnson, Spark and Fowles is concerned, however, with a fairly restricted notion of absence. Although characters are paraded as fictions, often this is in order to suggest that we are all, *metaphorically*, fictions. This can even be reassuring: an affirmation of a substantial everyday world, however much we operate in terms of its metaphorical extensions. The 'disturbance' in a novel like Nathalie Sarraute's *The Golden Fruits* (1963) is much more extreme. Here the readings of *The Golden Fruits* by the readers in *The Golden Fruits* is the novel we are reading. The subject of the book is its non-existence outside its own repetitions. As the characters read the book we are reading, the text continually turns its own third-person narrative into a first-person discourse. The 'I' continually turns the 'he' into a 'you' in his or her *sous-conversation*. As the novel opens, for example:

> the earth opens up. Enormous crevasse. And he, on the other side walking away without turning round . . . he should come back . . . don't abandon us . . . towards you . . . with you . . . on your side . . . take hold of what I'm throwing you. . . . Tell me have you read? . . . what did you think of it? (p. 11)

Desiring communication which is impossible because the level of narration is separate from the level of story, the 'I' attempts to treat the text itself as an addressee. This coming together of speaker and text is described as if they were lovers: 'We are so close to each other now, you are so much a part of me that if you ceased to exist, it would be as if a part of me had become dead tissue' (p. 142). The irony is that the text, of course, *is* the speaker, and vice versa. Like 'star-crossed lovers', they are dependent upon each other for existence (a more radically metafictional treatment of the problem examined in Johnson's *Christie Malry's Own Double Entry*).

However, some British and American writing does, like Sarraute's, operate metafictionally at the level of the sign. In John Barth's 'Autobiography: A Self-Recorded Fiction' (to which a note is added: 'the title "Autobiography" means self-composition: the antecedent of the first person narrator is not I but the story speaking of itself. I am its father, its mother is the recording machine'; *Lost in the Funhouse*, p. 1), the story explicitly discusses its own 'identity' crisis. This involves its defects – 'absence of presence to name one' (p. 38) – and its attempts to 'compose' itself (p. 36), given these defects.

Gabriel Josipovici's *Moebius the Stripper* (1974) directly confronts the problem of absence by reproducing the text typographically in the form of a representation of a Möbius strip and exploring the crisis of Möbius, who has to die for the story to become text, who of course depends on the story for existence, but who cannot exist *because* of the story.

What the various fictional examples of this chapter suggest, in fact, is the extent to which the dominant issues of contemporary critical and sociological thought are shared by writers of fiction. This reveals, as one critic has said, that:

the case of being trapped inside an outworn literary tradition may be taken as a special symptom of the feeling that we are all trapped in our systems for measuring and understanding the world: that in fact there is no 'reality' except our systems of measuring.

(Forrest-Thompson 1973, p. 4)

The next chapter will examine the nature of this 'outworn literary tradition' and the centrality of metafictional writing in its renewal.

3

Literary evolution: the place of parody

The development of the novel

How can metafiction be 'placed' within the evolution of the novel, as well as within the context of non-literary culture, and still be seen as a point of renewal rather than a sign of exhaustion? Ultimately, questions about the viability of metafiction lead to questions about the viability of the novel itself and its possible future development.

Such questions can only be examined through some consideration of how literary genres develop or become exhausted. Hayden White argues that literary change of a generic nature reflects changes in the general social-linguistic codes and that these reflect changes in this historico-cultural context in which a given language game is being played. This certainly supports the view suggested here so far. He goes on to argue that writers may, in any given period, experiment with different systems of encoding and decoding, but

a given period of such experimentation will find an audience 'programmed' to receive innovative messages and contacts only if the sociocultural context is such as to sustain an audience whose experience of that context corresponds to the modes of message formulation and conveyance adapted by a given writer. Significant literary changes, then, can only take place at times when the audiences are so constituted as to render banal or unintelligible the messages and modes of contact of those preceding.

(White 1975, p. 108)

To be successfully decoded, then, experimental fiction of any variety requires an audience which is itself self-conscious about its linguistic practices. These conditions are surely provided by the contemporary attention to communication problems, to the rise of new commercial and technological languages that cannot be translated into the terms of more familiar linguistic codes. This audience, however, has its own requirements. The forms and language of what is offered to it as creative or experimental fiction should not be so unfamiliar as to be entirely beyond the *given* modes of communication, or such fiction will be rejected as simply not worth the reading effort. There has to be some level of familiarity. In metafiction it is precisely the *fulfilment* as well as the *non-fulfilment* of generic expectations that provides both familiarity and the starting point for innovation. The well-worn conventions of realism or of popular fiction are used to establish a common language which is then extended by parodic under-mining and often amalgamated with cultural forms from out-side the mainstream literary tradition, including journalese, television influences such as soap opera, cinematic devices and the effects of such genres as space opera.

Some critics maintain that the 'death of the novel' has occurred as the result of suffocation and dislocation by these popular cultural forms. This, to some extent, accounts for the critical refusal to accept that if the novel does *not* meet these challenges then it will become obsolescent. Added to this, however, is an essentially negative view of the parodic basis of much contemporary writing – in particular, metafiction – whereby parody is regarded as inward-looking and decadent. In fact, parody in metafiction can equally be regarded as another lever of positive literary change, for, by undermining an earlier set of fictional conventions which have become automa-tized, the parodist clears a path for a new, more perceptible set. The problem arises because parody is double-edged. A novel that uses parody can be seen either as destructive or as critically evaluative and breaking out into new creative possibilities.

The most positive view both of parodic devices and of the integration of popular forms within the development of a literary genre is provided by the Russian formalist theory of literary evolution. If metafiction is to be viewed optimistically from both cultural and formal perspectives, Russian formalist theories offer valuable insights. It is useful anyway to look more closely at the specifically *literary* system to discover to what extent generic change may be brought about by internal pressures (see Bennett 1979).

Russian formalist theory begins with Viktor Shklovsky's notion of *ostranenie* or defamiliarization.[6] Literature here becomes a means of renewing perception by exposing and revealing the habitual and the conventional. This leads Shklovsky to the second main concept in his theory, that of 'laying bare the device' in order to achieve defamiliarization. Literature can thus be seen as inherently self-conscious, for 'laying bare the device', when applied to the literary work itself, results in self-conscious parody. In the Russian formalist terms of literary evolution, however, such parody would be seen as a point of positive renewal in literary development, for the concept of 'making strange' or defamiliarization implies a literary dynamism: things cannot *remain* strange. In these terms, therefore, metafiction represents a response to a crisis within the novel – to a need for self-conscious parodic undermining in order to 'defamiliarize' fictional conventions that have become both automatized and inauthentic, and to release new and more authentic forms. Parody, as a literary strategy, deliberately sets itself up to break norms that have become conventionalized.

Russian formalist theory can thus be seen to offer an optimistic view of metafictional strategies within the evolution of the novel. And this optimism can be strengthened by considering one of the other main strands of formalist theory: the notion of literature as a system that develops itself through the realignment of units *within* that system, and through its absorption of elements *outside* the literary system. Apparently obsolete devices, which have been relegated to the level of the 'popular', are, in this view, repeated in a new and often incongruous context and made to function again. Although the notion of 'high art' remains, therefore, it becomes a dynamic category which constantly redefines itself through the popular and the non-literary. Metafiction explicitly and self-consciously performs these functions, for it seeks to avoid a radical break with previous 'literary' traditions. Instead it 'lays them bare' and realigns the still viable components with elements considered to be 'popular', but perhaps also having extreme relevance for a contemporary readership. At present this might include, for example, the spy thriller, the family saga, the space opera, science fiction and the historical romance.

Later formalist theory reveals the extent to which Shklovsky's formalist concentration has an implicit historical dimension. If literature deviates from a norm in order to renew perception, and has therefore continually to change its structures, then the older literary norm necessarily constitutes the 'background' against which the new textual innovations foreground themselves and can be understood. The problem at present is that there is no commonly agreed norm to provide a background. The norm has therefore to be made *explicit* as a literary structure – as the basis for parody – within the contemporary text, instead of remaining a set of *implicit* cultural and literary codes which are activated by the reader in the reading process. In reading metafiction, then, where the literary norm(s) become the object of parody, the reader is educated in the relationship of historical and cultural to literary systems. Parody of an earlier literary norm or mode unavoidably lays bare the relations of that norm to its original historical context, through its defamiliarizing contextualization within a historical present whose literary and social norms have shifted. Parody of a literary norm modifies the relation between literary convention and cultural-historical norms, causing a shift in the whole system of relations. Certainly Juri Tynyanov's work (Tynyanov 1971) suggests that a text is 'literary' depending on its differential relation to the extra-literary system in which it operates. In focusing on the issue of 'literariness', metafiction examines the relations between literary and historical systems and, at the very least, implicitly historicizes literary tradition.

So, in metafiction, a convention is undermined, or laid bare, in order to show its historical provisionality: to show, for example, that the use of an implicitly male omniscient author in popular continuations of realism is tied to a specific ideological world-view which continues insidiously to pass itself off as 'neutral' or 'eternal' or 'objective', and which has its historical roots in the late eighteenth and early nineteenth centuries. Russian formalist theory helps to show how parody and the assimilation of the 'popular' or the 'non-literary' (which ultimately breaks down distinctions between 'high' and 'low' art and reveals the terms in which they are set up) can promote a very positive and long-overdue renewal of the novel, rather than its exhaustion. Metafictional parody reveals how a particular set of contents was expressed in a particular set of conventions recognized as 'literature' by its readers, and it considers what relevance these may still have for readers situated at a different point in history. It exploits the indeterminacy of the text, forcing the reader to revise his or her rigid preconceptions based on literary and social conventions, by playing off contemporary and earlier paradigms against each other and thus defeating the reader's expectations about both of them.

The use of parody and the assimilation of popular and non-literary languages in metafiction thus helps to break both aesthetic and extra-aesthetic norms. because both languages operate through very well-established conventions, however, the reader is able to proceed through the familiar to the new. The text is freed from the 'anxiety of influence' (Bloom 1973) by the paradoxical recognition that literature has never been free, cannot be 'original', but has always been 'created' or produced. The reader is freed from the anxiety of meaninglessness by the recognition that not only can literature never be free in terms of literary tradition; it also cannot be free either in its relation to the historical world or in its relation to readerly desire.

The novel, always inherently self-conscious, always inherently provisional in its process of relativizing language through continuous assimilation of discourses, has now and again to stop and examine the process, to see where it is going, to find out what it is. Throughout its history, of course, the implicit tendency of the novel to draw attention to its linguistic construction has emerged, 'now and again', as the dominant function in individual works: in *Tristram Shandy*, for example, or in Jane

Austen's *Northanger Abbey* (1818). In contemporary metafictional writing, not only is such self-consciousness the dominant
function within *individual* novels of the type; it is clearly emerg-
ing as the dominant characteristic of the contemporary novel *as
a whole*. I would argue that at present the novel is coping with its
most major crisis. However, its strong tendency towards self-
consciousness has quite clearly led already, not to a decline or a
'death', but to a renewed vigour.

The method of parody: creation plus critique

> In truth parody was here the proud expedient of a great gift
> threatened with sterility by a combination of scepticism,
> intellectual reserve and a sense of the deadly extension of the
> kingdom of the banal.
>
> (Thomas Mann, *Dr Faustus*, p. 148)

Parody fuses creation with critique to replace, as one observer
has remarked, what had become 'a matter of course' with what
now becomes a 'matter of discourse' (Stewart 1979, p. 19). The
specific method of parody, the actual process involved in this
substitution, has been usefully explained as:

> a kind of literary mimicry which retains the form or stylistic
> character of the primary work, but substitutes alien subject
> matter or content. The parodist proceeds by imitating as
> closely as possible the formal conventions of the work being
> parodied in matters of style, diction, metre, rhythm, vocabul-
> ary.
>
> (Kiremidjian 1969, p. 232)

In other words, parody renews and maintains the relationship between form and what it can express, by upsetting a
previous balance which has become so rigidified that the conventions of the form can express only a limited or even irrelevant
content. The breaking of the frame of convention deliberately
lays bare the process of automatization that occurs when a
content totally appropriates a form, paralysing it with fixed
associations which gradually remove it from the range of cur-

rent viable artistic possibilities. The *critical* function of parody thus discovers which forms can express which contents, and its *creative* function releases them for the expression of contemporary concerns. Parody has, of course, always performed these functions: Walter Shandy's hovering foot, for example, in *Tristram Shandy* (1760), is on one level a *direct critique* of the mimetic fallacy of Richardson's exhaustive attention to detail. On another level, however, it provides a more *general insight* into the very essence of narrative – its inescapable linearity, its necessary selectiveness as it translates the non-verbal into the verbal – and finally *creates* its own comedy out of its critique. However, because parody has been considered mainly as a form of criticism, it has been regarded as a sign of generic exhaustion.

These functions of parody can be understood in terms of Jakobson's definition of the aesthetic funcion as a focus upon the message for its own sake, but with the 'message' here involving the *whole* literary system. Jakobson argued that the poetic function 'projects the principle of equivalence from the axis of selection into the axis of combination' (Jakobson 1960): in other words a metaphoric substitution is forced into an ongoing metonymic plane (see Lodge 1977a, pp. 88–93, for a critique of this definition). This is precisely what parody does. Taking as its starting point a previous work or genre, it inserts a metaphoric version of this into the ongoing (metonymic) literary tradition. This dislocates both past and present texts: the rearrangement of the original text or genre reveals the potential rearrangements of the present one. John Fowles's *The French Lieutenant's Woman*, for example, 'rewrites' the Victorian realistic novel and the historical romance but also explicitly offers itself as one out of *many* possible 'versions'.

In fact, new developments in fiction have always tended to evolve through the parody of older or outworn conventions. There has always been an 'Is the Novel Dead?' debate, in this sense, and it could be argued that the Novel *began* the formulation of its identity through parody. As one critic has said:

the devices of parody are absorbed into the valances of the new form as though the stammering novelist had first to lisp his alphabet in mocking echo of what he said in order to pronounce his own word. In this sense the novel has always been involved with parody to some degree.

(Rovit 1963, p. 80)

Cervantes' *Don Quixote* (1604) parodied the outmoded conventions of the Romance. Fielding broke away from Richardson's psychologically oriented detailism to create his panoramic comedies by parodying *Pamela* (1740) in *Shamela* (1741) and *Joseph Andrews* (1742). In *Shamela*, Fielding parodies the moral dubiousness of *Pamela* by imitating the epistolary form but using it to establish the foundation in inconsequentiality of the exalted sentiments of Richardson's text. Particularly with *Joseph Andrews*, however, he goes beyond a mere critique of Richardson's style and moral norms to establish his own, based on the virtues of the good heart in relation to a benign Providence. The parody of the novel of sensibility thus provides the starting point for the development of the 'epic' or 'panoramic' novel and establishes the two mainstreams of English fiction.

Only a few years after their initiation, both were being parodied in Laurence Sterne's *Tristram Shandy* (1760), which, as I have argued, can be seen as the prototype for the contemporary metafictional novel. Viktor Shklovsky referred to it as the most 'typical' novel, and it does, of course, base its metafictional subversion on the laying bare of the most fundamental set of all narrative conventions: those concerning the representation of time. Throughout the novel there is a continuous displacement of normal causal narrative sequence, which explicitly illustrates the process of retardation, the withholding of the final resolution, fundamental to all narrative. Such displacements lay bare the relations in fiction between what Shklovsky referred to as *fabula* and *sujet* – more recently Genette's *histoire* and *discours*: the nearest equivalent in English would be 'story' (the raw material, if it had existed) and 'plot' (the shaping of that material) (see note 5). *Tristram Shandy* is thus thoroughly a novel about itself, thoroughly 'aesthetic' in Shklovsky's use of the term, a novel about the transformation of its 'story' into 'plot'.

The basic strategy of the novel is retardation through incompletion. At all levels of *Tristram Shandy*, nothing is completed. Walter's encyclopaedia is never written. The novel begins with a description of the coitus interruptus which brings Tristram into the world. The central narrative is never finished because it is continually punctuated by descriptions of events whose relevance to the main story is apparent only to Tristram himself. Characters are repeatedly 'frozen' in time, stranded in odd voyeuristic poses at keyholes, or left in strange physical positions.

Subjective time continuously assimilates external events. The undermining of time is itself undermined by the subjectivism of a novel 'written' by a narrator desperately trying to catch up with himself and dissolving all events into the present of his discourse. The subject of the novel becomes the battle between the chronological duration of the 'writing' and that of the events in 'history', and the battle between these and the real and implied chronological duration of the reading. Historical dates have significance within patterns of personal rather than world history.

Trapped within the sequential, the closer language attempts to come to 'life' (to the actual relations of things in space-time) the further away and the more regressive it appears: 'the more I write the more I shall have to write' (p. 230). Writing develops as a problem of compound interest. When there is explicitly no fixed point of origin or reference, then digression becomes progression, and identity escapes. When events which are looked forward to on the level of the *histoire* have already been narrated by the *discours*, then 'history' becomes a non-category, and past and future in novels is shown to be merely (on one level) the before and after of the order of the *narration*.[7]

Parody appears again and again at points of crisis in the development of the novel. In *Northanger Abbey*, for example, Jane Austen parodies the gothic novel and in so doing sets up a dialogue about the function of novels which initiates her own form of comedy of manners, itself dependent upon a large measure of *self-parody* concerning the definition of 'good sense'. The phenomenon seems to be paralleled in the personal development of novelists themselves. Doris Lessing wrote *The Golden Notebook* (with its continual parodies of style and its 'Free Women' outer frame which parodies conventional realism) to resolve a personal crisis in her development as a writer: a 'writer's block' caused by her feeling that subjectivity is inauthentic; 'but there was no way of not being intensely subjective' (pp. 12–13). She finally achieves, through the critical function of parody, what a lot of women writers were later to achieve through the women's movement: creative release in her realization that 'writing about oneself is writing about others'.

John Barth's work *Chimera* (1972) is another response to a writer's block which is resolved through the process of writing about it: 'the key to the treasure is the treasure' (p. 56). Barth realizes the possible value of myth as a way out of the sterility and inauthenticity of realism:

> Since myths themselves are among other things poetic distillations of our ordinary psychic experience and therefore point always to daily reality, to write realistic fictions which point always to mythic archetypes is in my opinion to take the wrong end of the mythopoeic stick. . . . Better to address the archetypes directly.
>
> (p. 199)

However, Bellerophon (the 'hero' in the novel, who also suffers from a writer's block) attempts an exact imitation of the myth and, instead of becoming a hero, becomes a parody of one. He becomes the story of himself: 'I'd become not a mythic hero, but a perfect reset' (p. 203), 'a number of printed pages in a language not untouched by Greek' (p. 307). Barth, though, by treating the myth parodically through his two middle-aged heroes, Perseus and Bellerophon, goes on to create his own original story and overcomes the problem of his writer's block.

Parody in metafiction may operate at the level of style or of structure. B. S. Johnson's novel *See the Old lady Decently* parodies the conventions of the history textbook and the tourist guide at a stylistic level in order to show how they are both very partial and limited means of suggesting the infinite variety of human history, and yet constitute our staple approach to the past as 'heritage'. He undermines their style mainly through ellipsis, which highlights features through their omission. (Again this is a widely used metafictional technique: Donald Barthelme's *Amateurs* (1976) uses it in a similar and equally effective manner.) The history textbook is heavily dependent on the use of nouns that appear to refer to real names and places: so, of course, is much realist fiction. Johnson often omits such nominatives. Sometimes he replaces them with pronouns which do not appear to relate directly to the nominatives within the text:

> They feasted in the Norman keep.   He built the chapel and the third king's house in the wall.   His son rebuilt the chapel.   This one was formerly the seat of the Earl of, based within the boundaries of   what is left of   what used to be the outlaw's favourite haunt, the Forest of.
>
> (p. 19)

A similar strategy involves a parody of the guidebook.

> From Pass, a couple of miles to the east, half a dozen glaciers can be seen at once, and so near that their green fissures are clearly. Light and shadow upon the cluster of peaks are magical in their changes at, or and the traveller who has looked up from the green to watch a snowstorm trailing its curtain across the crests, with, perhaps a white summit standing serene above the cloud will not readily. Wooded but infertile are the most magnificent pastures.
>
> (p. 34)

This preserves the essential stylistic features of the original form. These include: generally a subject–verb–object construction or a passive, hence impersonal, form. There is liberal use of colour adjectives; continual modification and qualification with much embedding of clauses to draw the reader into the scene; heavy use of the pathetic fallacy, such as summits standing serene, a snowstorm 'trailing its curtain'. The aim of this is to envelop the reader in an idyllic, neatly humanized world which unfurls itself in orderly fashion.

The omission of locating nominatives, therefore, the overt contradiction of the last sentence, the gradual descent into incomprehensibility as the gaps become harder to fill, and the absurd use of anthropomorphism, emphasize that this is not only a *humanly* but also a *verbally* ordered 'natural' scene. It is an essay in rhetorical and commercial persuasion rather than a 'true' transcript. Yet the guidebook, with its own aim of appealing to as many tastes as possible, merely exaggerates the methods of all prose discourse in making the specific carry the general implications of a particular ideology. Here this is laid bare as the height of generality is achieved by the complete omission of the substantial. As a result the reader appears to have total freedom to substitute individual needs and desires. Johnson thus manages, through syntactical disruption, to convert the apparently 'objective' language of history into a postmodernist comment on the writing of history.

More commonly, metafiction parodies the *structural* conventions and motifs of the novel itself (as in *Tristram Shandy*) or of particular modes of that genre. Thus Muriel Spark uses the omniscient-author convention, not benevolently to signpost the reader's way through the text, but to express a disturbing authority whose patterns are not quite so easy to understand. David Lodge in *How Far Can You Go?* (1980) also flaunts this convention. The author steps into the text and refers to himself in a list of characters, nervously reminding the reader that he has labelled each character with a recognizable trait, so that their fortunes might more easily be followed. This reverses the effect of heightened credibility and authority usually attributed to the convention, and expresses formally some of the doubts and concerns expressed thematically, in the text, about sexual morality and finally the Catholic Church itself.

A metafictional text which draws on a whole plethora of parodistic effects, both stylistic and structural, is Doris Lessing's *The Golden Notebook*. The novel uses parody both to achieve a comic effect by exposing the gap between form and content, and to reveal frustration and despair. The novel is constructed from five notebooks, divided into four sections, each 'framed' by a section of a novel called 'Free Women', which also provides the outermost frame of *The Golden Notebook* itself. Everything in the text is apparently written by the central protagonist. Anna Freeman is searching for a means of fixing and relating her several identities – as woman, writer, mother, lover, communist – and she decides to separate them out into different notebooks, each written in a different style. She comes to realize, however, that her experiments with style serve only to undermine it as a reality-defining concept, and she is finally saved only by her recognition of an insight very well expressed in John Barth's *The End of the Road* (1958):

> to turn experience into speech – that is to classify, to catego-
> rize, to conceptualize, to grammatize, to syntactify it – is
> always a betrayal of experience . . . but only so betrayed can it
> be dealt with at all and only in so dealing with it did I ever feel
> a man alive and kicking.
>
> (p. 116)

'Free Women', the 'realistic' novel which Anna writes, based on the experiences of the notebooks, is precisely such an expression of the need for categorization to preserve sanity. However, the novel as a whole (and particularly the fifth notebook, into which all the others finally break down, the Golden Notebook) shows 'truth' to reside in muddle and breaks out of this constricting outer frame. Anna reflects:

> The essence of neurosis is conflict. But the essence of living
> now, fully, not blocking off what goes on, is conflict. In fact
> I've reached the stage where I look at people and say – he or
> she, they are whole at all because they've chosen to block off
> at this stage or that. People stay sane by blocking off.
>
> (p. 456)

But they live – which is true sanity – by not doing so. Lessing's novel itself exists within these terms, allowing some of the 'essence of living now' to escape the necessary novelistic formal 'blocking off'.

The parody throughout *The Golden Notebook* expresses the division its heroine feels within herself. It also expresses her desire for 'wholeness, for an end to the split, divided, unsatisfactory way we all live' (p. 171). Her search is partly for a reconciliation of the woman Anna with the artist Anna. For her Jungian analyst, Mother Sugar, this role conflict can only be resolved through the submergence of the individual self into the collective unconscious by means of the artistic process. But Anna as woman cannot accept this sacrifice of self. She loses faith in the ordering possibilities of art and language and increasingly experiences dreams which share 'the same quality of false art, caricature, parody' (p. 238). Anna comes to learn that *all* representation involves some parody, but she has further to learn to distinguish between the authentic parody of true art and the false representations of inauthentic art. 'Free Women', the novel she writes, is the ironic end of self-discovery. In its parody of realism, its revelation of the extent of the inadequacy of realist writing, it also represents the ironic end of self-discovery for Doris Lessing the novelist.

The inauthenticity of realism as 'analysis after the event' (p. 231) is even more thoroughly exposed in this frame than in the Yellow Notebook. The latter represents a sort of halfway stage in the petrification of 'experience' as it is mediated through the form of the traditional realist novel. In the Yellow Notebook, Anna offers a more stereotypical, fictionalized version of herself (Ella). This allows her to draw on the conventions of popular romance or of the agony column to explore aspects of personality that she cannot face directly in the Blue Notebook, her diary. 'Free Women' is the final stage of 'petrification'. This 'frame' *overtly* parodies the conventions of realism. It offers an apparently well-made plot and well-placed climax. Characters are introduced through formal case-histories. The 'divided self' theme is presented discursively and analytically. The frame presents a wholly dissatisfying version of Anna's experience. It is clearly a deliberate aesthetic strategy on Doris Lessing's part to 'lay bare' the conventions of realism as entirely inadequate vehicles for the expression of *any* contemporary experience and, in particular, the experience of women.

The structure of 'Free Women' is circular, beginning and ending in a room with Molly and Anna. Even this is exposed in its inauthenticity by the novel as a whole. Experience does not describe perfect circles. If anything, *The Golden Notebook* is conical in shape. The notebooks begin with the historical events set in the vast South African plains of the Black Notebook and end in a small room in the present of writing about the individual self.

In terms of the narrative order of the novel, 'Free Women' is presented first (though last in the supposed chronological order of the events), recording external, refined annihilated experience. The Black Notebook then presents the rejection of the past. It reveals the fallibility of memory and offers parodic versions of a novel previously written by Anna, 'Frontiers of War', about her South African experience. This novel is now rejected as unhealthily 'personal' and obsessive. The Red Notebook develops Anna's sense of public self-betrayal in her growing disillusionment wth the Communist Party. The Yellow Notebook presents a consciously fictive and parodic account of recent events in Anna's private life. The Blue Notebook attempts to reconcile past and present Annas through a diary account which becomes implicitly parodic. Finally the reader is taken into the Golden Notebook which is 'inside' Anna. Here, parody and representation are accepted as the same process.

Within each notebook there is also a gradual breakdown into a more personal vein, large-scale political and social concerns coming to focus on a single individual in each case. The Blue and Gold, the two 'personal' notebooks, become more complex and creative, full of textures, colours and imagery that relates the inner to the outer world. Stylistic homogeneity replaces the previous swing from detached analysis to near-hysteria. Time breaks down, becomes confused, as in Martha Quest's breakdown in Lessing's *The Four-Gated City* (1969).

The *breakdown* of Anna, of the novel form itself, is presented consciously in the terms of R. D. Laing's *breakthrough*. Just as Anna, in these terms, can only become whole by 'going down' into herself, so the novel performs the same act of subversion. The reader is forced to enter the process of the construction and breakdown of this fiction. Through the stylistic dislocation, the parody of social and fictional convention, he or she experiences the enlightenment and creative release provided by all successful parody. On one level, of course, the novel is a failure. Doris Lessing has not yet formulated a viable alternative to the traditional novel, nor a viable alternative politics to the male-defined discourses of the Communist Party. She does, however, 'lay bare' their inadequacies and thereby achieves a measure of release which breaks her own writer's block.

This 'release' function is central to parody, and therefore to metafiction. It operates on textual, psychological, generic and historical levels. Certainly what Freud argued for the release potential of the joke could be argued for parody. In *Jokes and their*

Relation to the Unconscious he shows that the power of jokes is a consequence of their form. As in dreams, this is based on a process of condensation plus substitution. He sees the function of jokes (as I have argued in the case of metafiction) as an extension of the play instinct. The parodist/metafictionist, using an established mode of fiction, lays bare the conventions that individual works of the mode share (which therefore define it) and fuses them with each other to extrapolate an 'essence'. This is then displaced through exaggeration and the substitution of a new content, so that the relationship of form to content, as in the joke, is itself laid bare. The joke, however, elicits only an immediate release response. Metafiction elicits both this *and* a release within the system of literary history.

> Freud argues further that what is special about jokes is their procedure for safeguarding the use of methods of providing pleasure against the objections raised by criticism which would put an end to the pleasure . . . the joke-work shows itself in a choice of verbal material and conceptual situations which will allow the old play with words and thoughts to withstand the scrutiny of criticism; and with that end in view every peculiarity of vocabulary and every combination of thought sequences must be exploited in the most ingenious possible way.
>
> (Freud 1976, p. 180)

In metafiction, the criticism is provided in the work itself by the process which produces the joke or parody, for this method of displacement and substitution carries with it an implicit critical function. Parody in metafiction, despite what its critics might argue, is more than a joke.

Metafictional novels are, of course, often regarded as 'escapist'. This is partly a consequence of their tendency to assimilate so-called 'escapist' popular forms. The last two sections have attempted to suggest how such novels are, in fact, extremely responsible both in socio-cultural terms and in terms of the development of the novel itself. It remains, therefore, to examine the popular forms upon which metafiction draws, and to answer the charges of escapism.

The use of popular forms in metafiction

The assimilation into mainstream fiction of 'fringe' or popular forms was an important feature of the Russian formalist view of literary evolution. It is a process which, like the parodistic impulse, has been given much prominence by writers of metafiction. Furthermore, the need to come to terms with popular forms can be seen as central to the survival of the novel as a widely read form of cultural expression. Roman Jakobson refined the Russian formalist concept of literature as a system and introduced the notion of 'shifting dominants' (see his essay 'The Dominant' in Matejka and Pomorska 1971). This involves the idea that what one age has considered to be trivial or of purely ephemeral entertainment value, another age will see as capable of expressing more profound anxieties and concerns. The entertainment value is still maintained, but the defamiliarization of the popular form within the new context uncovers aesthetic elements that are appropriate for expressing the serious concerns of the new age.

Thus the thriller, for example, may be regarded as 'popular' because of its stereotypical characters, plot and situations, escapism and often sensationalism, and its simplistic moral affirmations. In an age of uncertainty, however, it can be seen to contain within its conventions the potential for the expression of a deep human ontological insecurity through its central image of a man or woman threatened and on the run. The spy thriller, in particular, has been defamiliarized in this way over the last ten years. In the work of the still essentially 'popular' Le Carré, for example, it becomes a vehicle, as in *Smiley's People* (1980), for conveying present political and moral insecurities, and expressing the isolation of liberal values in a world of professionalization and amoral systems. It is not in its concerns so very far removed from the parodistic treatment of the same issues in Thomas Pynchon's *The Crying of Lot 49* (1966), a novel whose standing as modernist or post-modernist might be debated, but whose status as 'literature' clearly is not.

The important point about the formalist concept of 'shifting dominants' is that these possibilities for serious analysis are actually inherent in the popular form. They are not *tagged on* to it in order to attract a 'thinking' audience, but are actually *discovered through* it by successive audiences. The dynamism of the aesthetic function in Russian formalist theory must not be overlooked. As Jan Mukařovský pointed out:

> the value of an artistic artefact will be greater to the degree that the bundle of extra-aesthetic values which it attracts is greater, and to the degree that it is able to intensify the dynamism of their mutual connection.[9]

Thus certain popular forms are more likely than others at particular times to be taken up as modes of serious expression. The choice depends upon each set of historical and cultural circumstances.

The critic Leslie Fiedler was one of the first to argue that, in order to survive, the novel must return to its origins in the popular forms of a collectivist folk ethic which can 'bridge the gap' between the 'notion of one art for the cultivated, the favoured few . . . and another sub-art for the "uncultured" ' (Fiedler 1975, p. 348). His notion of popular forms is somewhat restricted, however. It is based less on an analysis of the function of literary formulae in relation to cultural expectations and readerly satisfactions than on the necessity for 'the machine age' to assimilate past traditions of fable and myth. His notion of 'popular culture' thus in many ways resembles Raymond Williams's 'culture that has been developed by a people', as opposed to 'a different kind of culture that has been developed for a people by an internal or external social group, and embedded in them by a range of processes from repressive imposition to commercial saturation; (Williams 1975, p. 128). Fiedler's view of culture similarly opposes a separation of 'high' and 'popular', unlike the cultural theory of, say, T. S. Eliot and F. R. Leavis.

Yet, in its implicit rejection of the technological base of much contemporary popular culture, Fiedler's position still perpetuates this division. Like Eliot and Leavis, he attempts to return to a pre-industrial homogeneous mythical past. The works of Angela Carter, Tom Robbins, Gerald Rosen and Robert Coover, however (writers who draw on the magical and the mythical but who rework popular fable in self-conscious and often metafictional ways), do provide examples that support

Fiedler's argument, and it is clear that such fiction has had a revitalizing influence on the novel as a whole.

In metafiction, though, writers experiment more commonly with the formulaic motifs of popular literary traditions which have often passed into cinematic forms of representation in the twentieth century: science fiction, ghost stories, westerns, detective stories, popular romance. Taking an 'archetypal structural' or Jungian view of this (a view ultimately not incompatible with Fiedler's), it could be argued that these forms are merely the different explicit historical shapes which manifest, at a surface level, archetypal desires that remain unchanged at a deep level. The familiar surfaces 'allow' for the expression of these desires (in Freudian terms) and are both socially acceptable and pleasurable. This view, however, ignores the continuous shift in historical consciousness at the level of both the everyday and the deeper social paradigm. At present, for example, there has been a shift involving an adjustment to *material* developments consequent upon huge technological expansion. There has also been an *ideological* shift involving the perception of reality as a construct (as discussed in Chapter 2).

J. G. Calvetti has defined a literary formula as a 'combination or synthesis of a number of specific cultural conventions with a more universal form or archetype'. This is 'useful primarily as a means of making historical and cultural inferences about the collective fantasies shared by large groups of people and for identifying differences in these fantasies from one culture or period to another' (Calvetti 1976, p. 7). The formula works by gradually imposing itself upon consciousness until it becomes the accepted vehicle of a particular set of attitudes, while allowing for a limited amount of individual variation. Like parody, therefore, the specific individual realizations of popular literary forms carry with them a continuous implicit *reference* to the collective base. Again like parody, they are in effect *self-referential*. Agatha Christie's novels, for example, appeal as much to the reader's experience of popular detective fiction as to his or her experience of the 'real world' outside it. Formulaic fictions thus construct ideologically powerful but intensely 'literary' worlds. They provide collective pleasure and release of tension through the comforting total affirmation of accepted stereotypes. What is interesting about their use in metafiction is that, when they are parodied, the release effect of such forms is to do with *disturbance* rather than *affirmation*. The reader is offered the temporary consolation of a release from contingency: the comfort of a total 'sense of an ending'. However, metafiction always simultaneously undermines such satisfactions and thereby reminds the reader of the necessarily, but not always apparent, selective restriction of *any* 'formulation'. Thus the reader may escape vicariously into the comforts of aesthetic certainty but he or she is certainly not allowed to rest complacently in this condition.

Probably the most formulaic of the popular fictional forms used in contemporary writing is the detective story. Todorov sees this as the masterpiece of popular literature because individual examples of the form most completely fit their genre (Todorov 1977, p. 43). Pure detective fiction is extremely resistant to literary change, and therefore a very effective marker of change when used explicitly against itself. Victor Shklovsky, in particular, was attracted by its almost exactly definable disposition of structural motifs, and he saw it as an obvious basis for studying plot.

In metafiction the detective-story plot is useful for exploring readerly expectation because it provides that readerly satisfaction which attaches to the predictable. Detective fiction is a form in which tension is wholly generated by the presentation of a mystery and heightened by retardation of the correct solution. Even characters, for the most part, are merely functions of the plot. Like metafiction, it foregrounds questions of identity. The reader is kept in suspense about the identity of the criminal until the end, when the rational operations of the detective triumph completely over disorder. Thus the reader enjoys the triumph of justice and the restoration of order, yet until the end he or she has been able to participate vicariously in the anarchic pleasure of the criminal's 'run'.

The detective story celebrates human reason: 'mystery' is reduced to flaws in logic; the world is made comprehensible. Pointing out that the high point of the pure form was reached during the high period of modernism (usually placed between 1910 and 1930), Michael Holquist has suggested that the detective story developed out of a need to escape the obsession with the irrational and the unconscious (Holquist 1971). However, in the post-modern period, the detective plot is being used to express not order but the irrationality of both the surface of the world and of its deep structures.

This is immediately apparent in the French New Novel. In Alain Robbe-Grillet's *La Jalousie* (1957), for example, the reader is reminded of a detective story by the way in which the narrative backtracks repeatedly to the same images, which thus seem to be offered as clues. They are clues, however, to a mystery which remains mysterious. No amount of obsessive and exasperated revisiting can discover their significance. They exist to reveal to the reader how enigma is generated in narrative. This, perhaps, is all their significance. The strongest code in Robbe-Grillet's fiction, as in all detective fiction, is what Roland Barthes has referred to as the 'hermeneutic' code 'through which an enigma is isolated, posed, formulated, delayed, finally resolved' (Barthes 1970, p. 26). In *La Jalousie*, though, the reader is not offered a resolution of the enigmatic dispositions of the text, and his or her attention begins to focus on *how* the code is constructed, *how* mystery is produced.

For writers like Borges, Nabokov and Spark, the hermeneutic code is ultimately a metaphysical one. Such writers use this supremely *rational* form of the novel in the service of the supremely *super-rational* (Borges, Spark), the *irrational* (Nabokov, Angela Carter) or the *anti-rational* (Fowles, Barthelme). In Spark's fiction, the hermeneutic code functions in reverse. The question 'What happens next?' is subordinated to the question 'Why did it happen?' through the fairly simple device of giving away the ending near the beginning of the narrative. The hermeneutic code is thereby translated into the terms of a metaphysical or moral enquiry (a technique also used very effectively in Marge Piercy's *Braided Lives* (1982) and *Woman on the Edge of Time* (1976), in John Irving's *The World According to Garp* (1976) and Fay Weldon's *Praxis* (1979)). This device of the 'flashforward' gives importance to apparently contingent details which are normally passed over in a first reading of a detective story. Such details normally only become significant in the light of knowledge of the ending, during a second reading.

In Spark's fiction they are rendered significant, however, in much more than the terms of narrative action. They become the vehicles of a moral and religious enquiry into the nature of 'absolute truth'.

Jorge Luis Borges uses an inversion of the detective story to expose the absurdity of faith in human reason in his story 'Death and the Compass' (1964). Like Agatha Christie's Poirot, his detective sets out to calculate by rational methods where the next murder in a series will occur, and by a twist of logic it emerges that he himself is the victim. As a good detective, he has total belief in the logical powers of the mind. He seeks 'a purely rabbinical explanation, not the imaginary mischances of an imaginary robber' (p. 106). Thus he fits together the clues with their (as he sees it) cabbalistic meanings to form a 'tetra-grammation' of time and space which allows him to foretell the time and location of the next murder. Every detail becomes a sign to be interpreted. Finally, in a state of semiotic intoxica-tion, he is led to the point where Scharlach fires the bullet. He discovers, too late of course, that he is the next victim. The reader is led to the full realization of the irony of constructing patterns and mistaking them for an ineluctable 'reality'.

The thriller is another form that provides a basis for such metafictional writing. John Hawkes, Thomas Pynchon, Muriel Spark, John Fowles, Italo Calvino and Anthony Burgess have all produced metafictional thrillers. Over recent years the spy thriller has undoubtedly become extremely popular. This is perhaps partly because of its suitability to television, but also, perhaps, because 'in detective stories, crime only threatens to destroy or upset a portion of society, whereas in the spy story civilization itself is undermined' (Harper 1969, p. 81). The thriller is based not upon the same faith in human reason as the detective story but much more upon the fear of anomie, of disorder, of the insecurity of human life. It is much closer to what appears to be the experience of living in the contemporary world. The spy, unlike the detective, but like contemporary men and women, does not know who he or she is looking for. The spy moves in a Kafkaesque world whose laws remain unknown. He or she is forced continually to shift identity, donning one disguise after another. The existential boundary situations that recur frequently in the thriller are experienced vicariously by the reader, who is thus allowed to play through the uncertainties of his or her own existence.

Harper suggests further of the thriller that its quality of delight is a mixed one: 'the exhilaration of freedom combined with fear and dizziness before the potential loss of self altogether' (ibid., p. 114). In Nabokov's *Pale Fire*, the thriller form is used experimentally to explore precisely the dizziness of a total loss of self. It is a comic exploration in many ways, because conveyed through the idiosyncratically expressed solipsism of the mad Kinbote (or is it Botkin?), the first-person narrator who may or may not be the King of Zembla. Kinbote has undertaken a detailed 'academic' commentary on John Shade's poem 'Pale Fire'. The poem appears to be a biography of Kinbote himself, who is really Charles the Beloved, the King of Zembla. Or is he? Or is the poem about him at all? Or is *everything* an invention not only of Nabokov himself but of an hallucinated psychotic? The 'shade' is introduced in the first lines of the poem winging its way in the 'reflected sky'. Reflections, forms of the double, have always been important in the thriller (and particularly in Nabokov's use of it: in *Despair* (1965) the protagonist commits a crime on the absurd assumption that a man who looks nothing like him is his double). Here, the possibility soon emerges that Kinbote's 'pursuer' may be his mad self whose projections are both the basis of, and inimical to, artistic invention, and which therefore destroy the poetic Shade.

Like Humbert Humbert in *Lolita* (1955), Kinbote's perversions appear to be confined to the sexual sphere. Both, however, are shown to pervert the artistic act in the manner in which they project their fantasies on to the world as 'realities'. the pursued 'exile' of the spy story is here primarily an 'exile' from himself. He is mad. Yet the irrationality of madness, of the uncertain world of the thriller, is contained within the supremely rational framework of the pedantic critical apparatus, the outer frame of the narrative. Again, the limitation of reason is exposed. Kinbote's footnotes to the poem appear to begin rationally but break down into irrational egotism. However, all along, and beyond reason, they testify to the truth of the fact that *every* interpretation is necessarily subjective, necessarily a reconstruction, a 're-reading'.

As Shade says, we should not refer to people as 'loony', since the term should not be applied to a 'person who deliberately peels off a drab and unhappy past and replaces it with a brilliant invention' (p. 188): a person such as a psychotic or an artist. Reason/unreason is shown as an inadequate dichotomization of life (hence the many allusions to Pope's *The Dunciad*), and the thriller form provides a very useful set of conventions for upending the normal application of such distinctions.

A full study of the use of popular forms by metafictional writers would have to include the use of romance (John Barth's *Sabbatical*, Margaret Drabble's *The Waterfall* (1969), Richard Brautigan's *The Abortion: An Historical Romance 1966* (1971)). It would have to include the use of science fiction (Thomas Pynchon's *Gravity's Rainbow*, Vonnegut's *The Sirens of Titan* (1959), Barthelme's 'Paraguay' (1970)). Motifs from pornographic writing often appear in metafiction novels employed to explore fundamental problems about human identity (Gore Vidal's *Myra Breckinridge* (1968), Brigid Brophy's *In Transit*, Robert Coover's 'The Babysitter'). The study might also look at the language of comic books (Clarence Major's *Emergency Exit* (1979), William Kotzwinkle's *The Fan Man* (1974)), the use of the family saga (John Irving's *The World According to Garp*, Vladimir Nabokov's *Ada* (1969)) and forms like the western (Richard Brautigan's *The Hawkline Monster: A Gothic Western* (1974).

These forms not only are entirely 'appropriate' as vehicles to express the serious concerns of the present day, but are forms to which a wide audience has access and with which it is already familiar. The use of popular forms in 'serious fiction' is therefore crucial for undermining narrow and rigid critical definitions of what constitutes, or is appropriately to be termed 'good literature'. Their continuous assimilation into 'serious fiction' is also crucial if the novel is to remain a viable form. Certainly the novels mentioned in this chapter have managed to bring together, very successfully, both the experimental and the innovative with the popular and the traditional.

4

Are novelists liars?
The ontological status of
literary-fictional discourse

'Truth' and 'Fiction': is telling stories telling lies?

What is the status, in philosophical terms, of 'universes' outside the domain of the everyday world? As Berger and Luckmann point out, for most people the everyday world is the only 'real' world: it is 'reality *par excellence*' (Berger and Luckmann 1971). 'It's common sense', 'I saw it with my own eyes', 'Seeing is believing', 'in touch', 'Out of sight, out of mind': all implicitly invoke the belief in such a common phenomenological world. Literary realism appears to be a continuation or extension of this 'commonsense' world. Authorial comments serve to reinforce its general 'truths' and continually refer the reader to the content of everyday reality. The language of realism is generally metonymic: descriptions are presented as a selection from a whole which is the real world.

Previous chapters have explored how, as one moves from realism through modernist forms to contemporary metafiction, the shift is towards an acknowledgement of the primary reality not of this 'commonsense' context of everyday reality but of the *linguistic* context of the literary text. This chapter will explore the philosophical implications of this ontological shift through an examination of the notion of 'context' offered by the metafictional text.

The meaning of an utterance in an *everyday* context is shaped
by this context:

> the historical 'context' of an utterance does not merely sur-
> round it but occasions it, brings it into existence. The context
> of an utterance, then, is best thought of not simply as its gross
> external or physical setting, but rather as the total set of
> conditions that has in fact determined its occurrence and
> form.
>
> (Smith 1979, p. 16)

The successful comprehension of a so-called 'natural utterance'
therefore depends on the resolution of indeterminacies of context. It depends upon the operation of the conventions of what
J. L. Austin has termed the 'appropriateness conditions' relevant to each speech-act context (Austin 1962). This will
include a variety of factors present in the immediate context: the
relation of speaker to hearer, tone of voice, paralinguistic
gestures, indexical reference to the immediate surround-
ings.

All written language, however, has to be organized in such a
way as to recreate a context or to construct a new context
verbally. All literary fiction has to construct a 'context' at the
same time that it constructs a 'text', through entirely *verbal*
processes. *Descriptions* of objects in fiction are simultaneously
creations of that object. (*Descriptions* of objects in the context of the
material world are determined by the existence of the object
outside the description.) Thus the ontological status of fictional
objects is determined by the fact that they exist by virtue of,
whilst also forming, the fictional context which is finally the
words on the page. Such language has to be highly conventional
in order to perform simultaneously the function of creating a
context and that of creating a text. Metafiction, in laying bare
this function of literary conventions, draws attention to what I
shall call the *creation/description* paradox which defines the status
of *all* fiction.

Metafictional writers differ among themselves, however, over
the precise relation of the verbal world of fiction to the everyday
world. Writers such as E. L. Doctorow, Vladimir Nabokov,
Muriel Spark, Iris Murdoch, Kurt Vonnegut suggest that

'reality' exists *beyond* 'text' certainly, but may only be reached *through* 'text', that

> History – Althusser's 'absent cause', Lacan's 'Real' – is *not* a text, for it is fundamentally non-narrative and non-representational; what can be added, however, is the proviso that history is inaccessible to us except in textual form, or in other words, that it can be appropriated by way of prior (re)textualisation.
>
> (Jameson 1981, p. 82)

Fiction is here a means of explaining a reality which is distinct from it, it is 'an instrument for finding our way about more easily in this world' (Vaihinger 1924, p. 15). Writers like Gilbert Sorrentino and Donald Barthelme, however, suggest that the only difference beween literary fiction and reality is that the former is constructed entirely with language and this allows certain freedoms. It means, for example, that

> These people aren't real. I'm making them up as they go along, any section that threatens to flesh them out, or make them 'walk off the page', will be excised. They should, rather, walk into the page, and break up, disappear.
>
> (Gilbert Sorrentino, *Imaginative Qualities of Actual Things* 1971, p. 27)

The everyday world is merely another order of discourse so that, as one of the characters in Donald Barthelme's novel *Snow White* (1967) says:

> The moment I inject discourse from my universe of discourse into your universe of discourse, the yourness of yours is diluted. The more I inject it, the more you dilute. . . .
>
> (p. 46)

Literary fiction simply demonstrates the existence of multiple realities.

So why the obsession with the possibility or the implications of the charge that 'telling stories is telling lies'? Certainly a Platonic concept of literature demands that imaginative freedom be morally justified. To the extent that this is a concern of all metafiction, its practitioners are Platonists. Telling stories may not, in fact, be telling lies, but until one has established the nature of 'truth' it will be impossible to know. So all metafictional novels have, finally, to engage with this question of the 'truth' status of literary fiction, and of necessity therefore with the question of the 'truth' status of what is taken to be 'reality'.

In attempting to define this ontological status of literary fiction, philosophers have traditionally fallen into two categories. First, there are the 'falsity' theorists, for whom fiction is clearly lies. Second, there are the 'non-referentiality' theorists (sometimes adopting the terms 'non-predication' or 'quasijudgement') who argue that it is simply inappropriate to talk about the 'truth' status of literary fiction. Some metafictional writers adopt these positions, but on the whole most have collectively constructed a third category, suggested by John Fowles's reference to fiction as 'worlds as real as, but other than the world that is. Or was' (*The French Lieutenant's Woman*, p. 86).

In the rest of this chapter, metafictional writing will be related not only to the first two positions but more particularly to the third position (referred to as the 'alternative worlds' theory). Metafictional texts explore the notion of 'alternative worlds' by accepting and flaunting the creation/description paradox, and thus expose how the construction of contexts is also the construction of different universes of discourse. The rest of this book will examine how and to what extent metafiction destabilizes 'commonsense' contextual constructions of the everyday world. It will examine how this is achieved by preventing the reader from settling into any given context and by making him or her aware of possible alternatives to this 'commonsense' reality.

Reference, naming and the existence of characters

Whatever their philosophical view of fiction, aestheticians and metafictional writers, in exploring the relations between 'fiction' and 'reality', all address themselves to two problems: first, the paradox concerning the identity of fictional characters; second, the status of literary-fictional discourse (the problem of referentiality). To take the first problem: a fictional character both exists and does not exist; he or she is a non-entity who is a somebody.

The speaker in John Barth's 'Night Sea Journey' (1968) thus cries out at the end of the story, when the dream is paradoxically accomplished:

> mad as it may be my dream is that some unimaginable embodiment of myself. . . will come to find itself expressing in however garbled or radical a translation, some reflection of these reflections. If against all odds this comes to pass, may you to whom, through whom I speak, do what I cannot: terminate this aimless brutal business.

> (p. 12)

Here is a character that is only a voice, having knowledge of its existence only, it appears, when it utters. Yet it has no power to stop the utterance. The embodiment longed for is of something outside language, beyond an author, but it is of course the author's 'voice' which is the utterance; language which is the totality of existence; text which is reality.

This paradox is a favourite one of Jorge Luis Borges. The narrator of 'The Other' (1975), an old man called Jorge Luis Borges, realizes that he is sitting on a bench next to his younger self and concludes that the younger self must have dreamt him. In another of Borges' *ficciones*, 'The Circular Ruins' (1964), a man dreams another man into existence. The dreamer is then terrified that this man might discover he is only an image, a character in a fiction, but then discovers that he himself has been dreamt into existence by the man. Throughout many metafictional novels, characters suddenly realize that they do not exist, cannot die, have never been born, cannot act.

Or they start to perform impossible acts. In Flann O'Brien's *At Swim-Two-Birds* the 'author' of the novel within the novel is tried by his characters while asleep for the injustices he has done to them. The characters at the end of Márquez's *One Hundred Years of Solitude*, and John Barth's *Sabbatical*, begin to write the novel we have just been reading. In Barth's novel *Letters* (1979), characters from Barth's other novels – Jacob Horner, Todd Andrews, Ambrose Mensch – write letters to themselves, to each other and to 'the Author'. One of the characters, who has previously read Barth's *The Floating Opera* and has met Todd Andrews, its hero, expresses reservations to the author, Mr B.: 'I felt a familiar uneasiness about the fictive life of real people and the factual life of "fictional" characters – familiar because, as I'm sure I have intimated, "I've been there before" ' (p. 58). Another character signs his name 'The Author', and the other characters then address him as 'Mr John Barth'.

Barth himself has commented in an interview:

> The tragic view of characterization is that we cannot, no matter how hard we try, make real people by language. We can only make verisimilitudinous people. That view itself is on the minds of the characters themselves in a novel like *Letters*. . . . I take the tragic view of the tragic view of character.
>
> (Quoted in Ziegler and Bigsby 1982, p. 38)

As linguistic signs, the condition of fictional characters is one of absence: being and not being. Fictional characters do not exist, yet we know who they are. We can refer to them and discuss them. Fictional characters who are narrators exist in the same condition:

> Through all the detours that on
> e wishes, the subject who writes will neve
> r seize himself in the novel: he will onl
> y seize the novel which, by definition, ex
> cludes him . . .
>
> (Raymond Federman, *Double or Nothing*,
> unnumbered page between 146 and 147)

Our statements about literary-fictional characters can be verified only by consulting the statements which *are* those characters, which have brought them into existence. Metafictional novels continually alert the reader to this consequence of the creation/description paradox. To make a statement in fiction is to make a character. All statements have 'meaning' in relation to the context in which they are uttered, but in fiction the statement is the character is the context. Thus characters in metafiction may explicitly dissolve into statements. They may act in ways totally deviant in terms of the logic of the everyday 'commonsense' world, but perfectly normal within the logic of the fictional world of which they are a part. They may travel in time, die and carry on living, murder their authors or have love affairs with them. Some may read about the story of their lives or write the books in which they appear. Sometimes they know what is going to happen to them and attempt to prevent it.

The question of the ontological status of fictional characters is ultimately inseparable from that of the question of the referentiality of fictional language. Both are fascinating to metafictional writers. Names in fiction refer to impossibilities that yet can be affirmed. We can refer to fictional characters by their names in the way that we refer to friends or relatives. However, as John Searle argues in *Speech Acts*, 'A proper name can only be a proper name if there is a genuine difference between the name and the thing named. If they are the same, the notion of naming and referring can have no application' (Searle 1969, p. 75). Searle might well now modify this statement, but it is still a useful way of pointing to the crucial fact that in fiction the description of an object brings that object into existence. In the everyday world the object determines the description. However much 'fiction' is seen as interchangeable with 'reality', the crucial difference remains that in *literary* fiction the world is entirely a *verbal* construct.

The use of names in traditional fiction is usually part of an aim to disguise the fact that there is no difference between the name and the thing named: to disguise this purely verbal existence. Metafiction, on the other hand, aims to focus attention precisely on the problem of reference. Here, proper names are often flaunted in their seeming arbitrariness or absurdity, omitted altogether (as in Nathalie Sarraute's work), or placed in an overtly metaphorical or adjectival relationship with the thing they name. Gilbert Sorrentino breaks into his novel *Imaginative Qualities of Actual Things* (1971) to comment on a character called Dick:

> The first thing you should know about Dick (Detective) is that he is given this impossible name in order that the reader may ascertain certain things about his character. Or in all events, one certain thing. Basically, he was a gatherer of information. (p. 217)

Names are used to display the arbitrary control of the writer, and the arbitrary relationships of language: Pynchon's Stencil, Benny Profane, Oedipa Maas; Beckett's Watt, Hamm, Krapp; Fowles's Ernestina Freeman, Sarah Woodruff; Lessing's Anna Freeman; Vonnegut's Billy Pilgrim. The degree of transparency in each case is dependent on the degree of adherence to realistic illusion. The technique is reminiscent of eighteenth-century fiction – Tom Jones, Roderick Random, Squire Allworthy – but is deployed explicitly to split open the conventional ties between the real and fictive worlds rather than to reinforce them by mapping out a moral framework. In metafiction such names remind us that, in *all* fiction, names can describe as they refer, that what is referred to has been created anyway through a 'naming' process.

'Falsity' and 'non-predication' theories

Searle argues that the 'principle of identification' establishes that, in order to exist, the object must be distinguishable from the speaker's utterance of it. This is the basis for his view that in fiction the proposition containing the reference cannot be said to be 'true', because the proposition that the object exists cannot be said to be true. This is broadly a 'non-predication' position. Such a view would argue that fictional statements do not 'really' refer but only appear to do so. Although linguistic signs normally denote the non-linguistic entities for which they are signs, this is not the case with literary fiction. Such theories begin to move towards an emphasis on the special nature of the relationship between utterance and context in fiction, the relations between word and word, rather than word and world:

> the difference between a sentence used as an actual assertion and the same sentence used as a mock assertion . . . is not mirrored in the syntactic or other features of the sentence. This difference is a matter of the purpose the receiver assumes the utterance to have.
>
> (Olsen 1978, p. 47)

To some extent nearly all metafictional writers are aware of this quasi-referential status of fiction. Some, however, choose to develop it in terms of an 'alternative reality' rather than privileging the 'everyday world' as the 'real reality'. Texts that consistently undermine every assertion with a reminder to the reader of its quasi-referential status must obviously occupy a 'non-predication' position. Such underminings thoroughly remove the fictional text from the context of 'common sense' and emphasize its special linguistic status.

In John Barth's story 'Lost in the Funhouse' (1968) almost every sentence is undermined and exposed as fictional. The text exists as a dialogue between the reader and different narrators about the validity of the conventions available for telling stories. After the description of a character, the reader is immediately informed: 'Descriptions of physical appearance and mannerisms is one of several standard methods of characterization used by writers of fiction' (*Lost in the Funhouse*, pp. 73–4). Even sentences that appear to be reliable sources of information are so stylized as to offer an implicit comment on realism:

> Peter and Ambrose's father, while steering the black 1936 la Salle Sedan with one hand, could with the other, remove the first cigarette from a white pack of Lucky Strikes, and, more remarkably, light it with a match forefingered from its book and thumbed against the flint paper without being detached.
>
> (p. 75)

A mundane action is thus represented in a highly parenthesized, adjectivized sentence, using long pronominal phrases and extremely long qualifiers. The effect of this is to lull the reader, not into acceptance of the scene as *real*, but into acceptance of its reality as *a sentence in a book*. As with Tristram Shandy's attempt to recount his life-story, progression is always digression. The attempt exhaustively to describe anything constructs not an illusion of that object but a reminder of the presence of language.

Similarly, Raymond Federman in *Double or Nothing* continually rehearses possible narrative strategies. The novel as a whole is a commentary on the practice of writing fiction, with a novelist inside it writing a novel which is a commentary on the practice of writing fiction. It is a demonstration of Roland Barthes's view of how a metalanguage can become in its turn the language-object of a new metalanguage (Barthes 1967). At each stage in the novel, the outer narrator, the 'noodleman', agonizes about the many possible ways of telling the story (which becomes the story of its telling):

FIRST PERSON

or

THIRD PERSON

FIRST PERSON is more restrictive   more subjective   more personal   harder

THIRD PERSON is more objective   more impersonal   more encompassing   easier

I could try both ways:

I was standing on the upper deck next to a girl called Mary . . . No Peggy

He was standing on the upper deck next to a girl called Mary . . . No Peggy

(comes out the same).

(*Double or Nothing*, p. 99)

Throughout *Double or Nothing* Federman also draws the reader's attention to the book as artefact through typographic experiment and manipulation of white space. Laurence Sterne's blank-page 'description' of the Widow Wadman is probably the most famous example of this. The 'description' serves to draw attention to the fact that what is described in the real world exists before its description. In fiction, if there is no description, there can be no existence.

B. S. Johnson uses a similar technique to remind the reader of the material existence of the book. In *Albert Angelo* (1964) a hole is cut into a page describing a routine conversation in a school staffroom. Through it, the reader perceives part of a passage describing Christopher Marlowe's death. Turning over the page, he or she discovers the description of a contemporary café brawl. There is also, however, *another* hole, further deferring the appearance of a context which will 'explain' the Marlowe passage. The reader is thus forced to reflect upon the conventions not only of narrative suspense (which works essentially by deliberately impeding the completion of the action or the explanation of a story, while gradually filling in 'blanks' in the text) but also of the contextual basis of 'meaning' both inside and outside fictional texts.

In G. Cabrera Infante's *Three Trapped Tigers* (1965), a section heading 'Some Revelations' is followed by four blank pages (pp. 280–3). In Ronald Sukenick's *Out* (1973), Federman's *Double or Nothing* and *Take it or Leave it* (1976), Christine Brooke-Rose's *Thru* (1975) and *Between* (1968), and William H. Gass's *Willie Masters' Lonesome Wife* (1968), the typographic arrangements on the page *visually* imitate the content of the story. Barthelme's 'At the Tolstoy Museum' (1970) reproduces a pencil sketch of Tolstoy, of his coat, of the museum. 'Brain Damage' (1970) presents the reader with pictorial images of disembodied heads and surrealistic rearrangements of the human body.

Elaborate introductions to the novel, footnotes, marginalia, letters to publishers – inclusion of the physical 'scaffolding' of the text – these again are reminders of the text's linguistic condition. Gilbert Sorrentino's *Mulligan Stew* (1979) begins with a series of parodic (?) letters written by editors who have rejected the novel for publication. Several of Vladimir Nabokov's novels begin in a similar fashion. *Lolita* begins with a foreword by John Ray (the friend of Humbert Humbert's lawyer), who completes the 'stories' of the personages in Humbert's story, beginning at the point where Humbert's story ends. The novel ends with a comment on the book by Nabokov himself. He admits that such a commentary may strike the reader as 'an impersonation of Vladimir Nabokov talking about his own books' (p. 328).

Although most of these writers draw attention to the 'quasi-referential' linguistic status of the fictional world, they also allow the reader to construct an imaginative reality out of those words. In its pure form a 'non-predication' position would be (and is) clearly restrictive. Philosophers who argue for a 'non-predication' position come up against the problem that it suggests that sentences in fiction are the same as those that predicate something to an obviously non-existent (nonsensical) person. Metafictional writers come up against the problem that, even if the text is purely a linguistic construct which does not 'hook on to' the real world, language in literature is at a secondary level of signification, words carry their everyday significances into fictional texts, and readers cannot be prevented from constructing imaginative worlds from these words based on their own 'everyday' experiences.

Even more restrictive, however, is the 'falsity' position. Philosophers who view literary fiction in this light would include Plato, David Hume, Bertrand Russell, Willard Quine and A. J. Ayer. Plato excluded it from his ideal state, dismissing it as lies. David Hume dismissed poets as skilful liars. For Russell, 'there are no unreal individuals, so that the null-class is the class containing no members, not the class containing as members, all unreal individuals' (Russell 1905, p. 491). For Quine, nothing exists that does not exist within the laws of time and space of the world that we inhabit.[10]

Fiction, though, is clearly not a case of simple falsehood. It does not *set out* to inform. Thus metafictional writers who attempt to view it in this light place upon themselves huge constraints which are ultimately extremely counter-productive. B. S. Johnson is a good example of a writer whose literal and obsessive application of the notion of fiction as lies became damaging to his work. He begins by attempting to write obsessively 'factual' autobiographical accounts 'to understand without generalization' (*The Unfortunates* (1969), unpag.). His aim is to discover an ideal language which could directly transfer his state of mind to the reader's. When this fails, he swings desperately into extreme, defensive, metafictional subversions of the text.

Occasionally he experiments with concrete poetry. It is as if he hopes, through the resemblance of signifier and signified in the iconic sign, to reduce the area of indeterminacy and potential misinterpretation. He also, of course, reduces the freedom of the reader. (Fiction is 'lies' for Johnson because it exists within the public medium of language. It therefore cannot be 'owned' by an 'author' who is its sole creator. Thus Johnson becomes a metafictionist through a frustrated romanticism.) Often he falls into a naïve imitative fallacy. His use of typographical experiment can be seen as a progression of the view expressed in *Travelling People* (1963) that 'the style of each chapter should spring naturally from its subject matter' (Introduction). Such techniques are probably used most successfully in *See the Old Lady Decently* (1975). Here (in a manner very similar to William

H. Gass's *Willie Masters' Lonesome Wife*) the arrangement of the letters 'mammarytit' in the shape of a female breast serves to provide a wider perspective on the main theme of the novel: motherhood, England as the motherland. The concrete form allows Johnson to focus simultaneously on the female shape, its biological maternal function, the idea of the Virgin Mary, the infantile phonetic representation of the word 'mother' and the demotic term for the breast.

Johnson's work represents his search for a lost 'sincerity', a truth to the inner human being which will correspond with what he perceives outside. What he discovers, though, is the *lack* of correspondence, the existence of what Borges describes in *A Personal Anthology* (1961): 'through the years a man peoples a space with images of provinces, kingdoms, mountains, bays, ships, islands, fishes, rooms. . . . Shortly before his death, he discovers that the patient labyrinth of lines traces the image of his own face' (p. 174). He discovers that 'life does not tell stories, life is chaotic, fluid, random; it leaves myriads of ends untied, untidily. Writers can extract a story from life only by strict, close selection, and this must mean falsification' (*Memoirs* (1973), p. 14).

What threatens to take over, as the gap between feeling and form grows inevitably clearer, is solipsism. As A. Alvarez has suggested, the desperate search for new forms makes 'the dredged up material more available' (Alvarez 1966, p. 73). In attempting to express it, the writer relives it, not under the controlled abreactive situation of psychotherapy, but under the pressure of an intense internalization. Johnson's discovery is that the ironic consequence of writing is its annihilation of what it attempts to 'represent'. He is a metafictionist second and a romantic first. He resembles the character Hugo in Iris Murdoch's *Under the Net* (1954). Both believe in the supremacy of the self and the incapacity of language to express that self. Like Hugo, Johnson also failed, tragically and inevitably, to get out from under a 'net' which increasingly closed in on him until his suicide. His work and life reveal the tragic potential in the assumption by a self-conscious writer of an extreme 'falsity' position.

'Alternative worlds' theories

Most metafictional writers, however, eschew both 'non-predication' and 'falsity' positions. They are self-consciously anxious to assert that, although literary fiction is only a verbal reality, it constructs through language an imaginative world that has, within its own terms, full referential status as an alternative to the world in which we live. Fictional statements exist and have their 'truth' within the context of an 'alternative world' which they also create. Statements in the real world have their 'truth' in the context of a world which *they* help to construct. Fiction is merely a different set of 'frames', a different set of conventions and constructions. In this view, a fictional character is 'unreal' in one sense, but characters who are not persons are still 'real', still exist, within their particular worlds. As William H. Gass suggests: 'Worlds? But the worlds of the novelist I hear you say do not exist. Indeed. As for that – they exist more often than the philosophers' ' (Gass 1970, p. 4).

Metafiction lays bare the linguistic basis of the 'alternative worlds' constructed in literary fictions. Through continual shifts in and therefore revelations of context, metafictional texts expose the creation/description paradox. The more a text insists on its linguistic condition, the further it is removed from the everyday context of 'common sense' invoked by realistic fiction. Metafictional texts show that literary fiction can never imitate or 'represent' the world but always imitates or 'represents' the discourses which in turn construct that world. However, because the medium of all literary fiction is language, the 'alternative worlds' of fiction, as of any other universe of discourse, can never be totally autonomous. Their linguistic construction (however far removed from realism they may be) always implicitly evokes the contexts of everyday life. These too are then revealed as linguistically constructed. As Umberto Eco points out in a discussion of 'possible worlds' (here referred to as 'alternative worlds'):

> No fictional world could be totally autonomous, since it would be impossible for it to outline a maximal and consistent state of affairs by stipulating ex nihilo the whole of its individuals and of their properties. . . . it is enough for a story

to assert that there exists an (imaginary) individual called
Raoul; then, by defining him as a man, the text refers to the
normal properties attributed to men in the world of reference.
A fictional text abundantly overlaps the world of the reader's
encyclopedia. But also, from a theoretical point of view, this
overlapping is indispensable, and not only for fictional
worlds.

(Eco 1981, p. 221)

Metafictional texts thus reveal the ontological status of all
literary fiction: its quasi-referentiality, its indeterminacy, its
existence as words and world. They may exaggerate the consequence of the creation/description paradox: that language in
fiction has to be carefully organized in order to construct
contexts which are more fully 'given' or assumed in the real
world. Such texts, however, emphasize that the ability to
manipulate and construct hypothetical, alternative or ontologically distinct 'worlds' is also a condition of social existence, of
life outside novels.

Because of the creation/description paradox, as Wolfgang
Iser points out: 'if the literary communication is to be successful
it must bring with it all the components necessary for the
construction of the situation, since this has no existence outside
the literary work' (Iser 1975, p. 21). Metafiction not only
exposes the inauthenticity of the realist assumption of a simple
extension of the fictive into the real world; it also fails *deliberately*
to provide its readers with sufficient or sufficiently consistent
components for him or her to be able to construct a satisfactory
alternative world. Frames are set up only to be continually
broken. Contexts are ostentatiously constructed, only to be
subsequently deconstructed.

At first glance, this might appear to be merely an extension of
an essentially modernist strategy. Novels with multiple narrators or points of view axiomatically shift context. In modernist
fiction, however, the reader may be *temporarily* dislocated when
point of view, for example, is shifted, but is allowed to reorient
him or herself to the new perspective and recontextualize each
new piece of discourse. Metafiction sets mutually contradictory
'worlds' against each other. Authors enter texts and characters
appear to step into the 'real' world of their authors. Words

self-consciously displayed as words appear to get up and walk off the page to haunt the author or argue with the reader.

In modernist texts such as *The Waves* (1931), *To the Lighthouse* (1927), *The Sound and the Fury* (1931), the contextual shifts can be 'naturalized' by the construction of a narrator whose ontologically non-problematical 'full' subjectivity gives significance to the discourse. The reader soon realizes that the incoherence of Benjy's discourse in *The Sound and the Fury* is a result of its restriction to a purely perceptual point of view, a lack of reflective consciousness. The complexities of Quentin's discourse, in the same novel, are the result of an excess of reflectiveness. The shift from one to the other causes some uncertainty about the nature of the 'reality' they perceive, but never any doubt whether it exists. The reader is given enough 'components' to construct a context for these discourses which stabilizes their meaning.

B. S. Johnson uses a similar technique throughout *House Mother Normal* (1971). Here the interior monologues of the nine old people are prefaced at each utterance with a dwindling intelligence count. In its 'scientific' accuracy, this provides the only stable context (albeit a highly abstract and dehumanizing one) for the increasingly meaningless monologues. However, the shifts can be recontextualized in terms of a hierarchy of provisional authorities: the individual characters, the scientific information, the author himself. What happens at the end, though, is a shift from modernist perspectivism to post-modernist doubt, for the house mother steps out of the frame of the world *in* the fiction to declare her reality in the world *of* the fiction: to declare her reality, therefore, as language, as B. S. Johnson's invention.

Up to this point, the text can be understood in terms of the modernist strategy of unreliable narration, where *histoire* and *discours* become discrepant. The reader makes sense of such narratives by recontextualizing the discrepancies at progressively higher levels of the text until an authoritative norm is discovered. This implicitly draws attention to the process of the construction of the 'world', but through *consciousness*. Postmodernist texts draw attention to the process of the construction of the *fictive* 'world' through *writing*. In texts that employ

such overtly metafictional strategies, final resolution can only
be through either an awareness of the linguistic reality of the
text itself or the acceptance of the existence of mutually exclusive realities or 'worlds'.

There are many texts, of course, which are borderline examples. D. M. Thomas's *The White Hotel* (1981) is, in the
manner of Nabokov's *Pale Fire*, 'about' interpretation. It offers
an array of textual devices so that the accoutrements of textuality – letters, documents, literary productions to be analysed,
footnotes, journals – become the text. Freud's correspondence,
the Gastein journal, the poem 'Don Giovanni', the case-history
of Frau Anna G., are discrepant 'interpretations' and manifestations of the neurotic symptoms of Elisabeth Erdman. The
final resolution of the textual contradictions, these essentially
interpretative shifts, is, however, effected through what may or
may not be a shift in the definition of reality involving Elisabeth's special 'psychic' powers, her historical foreknowledge.
The 'symptoms' which Freud explains by reconstructing Elisabeth's *personal* past turn out to be her intimation of future
historical events in relation to her *racial* identity as a Jew. The
future is revealed through a documentary account of the Babi
Yar massacre and a vision of the 'New Jerusalem' which Lisa
discovers after death.

Unlike *Pale Fire*, however, within the novel *The White Hotel*
there is no ambiguity about the fact that this place, 'the camp',
exists. Within a 'commonsense' order of discourse, the possibility of clairvoyance and the possibility of life after death are not
unusual assumptions. The reader does not have to solve the
contradictoriness of the narrative shifts through a recourse to
the linguistic status of the worlds constructed through the
narrative. He or she does, however, have to recognize the
ontological flexibility of the norms of the 'everyday' world. It is
thus possible to read *The White Hotel*, by means of a modernist
aesthetic, as a text which foregrounds uncertainty about our
perception of the world; or to read it perhaps as a post-
modernist text which foregrounds uncertainty about its 'reality'
status through a flaunting of its condition of textuality and its
ostentatious construction of 'alternative worlds'.

Worlds of words: history as an alternative world

Metafictional novels allow the reader not only to observe the textual and linguistic construction of literary fiction, but also to enjoy and engage with the world within the fiction. For the duration of the reading at least, this world is as 'real' as the everyday world. Such novels reveal the duality of literary-fictional texts: all fiction exists as words on the page which are materially 'real', and also exists in consciousness as worlds created through these words: 'the aesthetic object belongs to the ideal but has its basis in the real' (Ingarden 1973, p. xxx). The reader is made aware that, in the fiction-reading process, an act of consciousness creates an 'object' that did not exist before. However, the reader is further reminded that this act cannot create anything that could exist outside the dialectic of text and consciousness (anything that has what Ingarden calls 'ontic autonomy', or demonstrates what Searle refers to as the 'principle of identification').

In *The Literary Work of Art* (1973), Ingarden suggests how realist texts are concretized, or produced, by readers. As in all literary fiction, the author projects, through quasi-judgemental statements, the 'states of affairs' which form the imaginary world. If the work were a 'real' historical or documentary account, the reader would match these with *determinate* individual states of affairs existing historically. However, in realism, the reader matches them with a *general type*, based on the particulars of a given historical time but not coincidental with them. Because of the similarity in the processes of constructing historical texts and realistic fictional texts, the practice is open to abuse. It could be argued that in realism one of these potential abuses is the appropriation and reduction of historical particularity for the support of assumptions about a timeless 'human nature' or a '*Plus ça change . . .*' philosophy.

There is a sub-category of metafictional novels which are particularly effective in foregrounding such abuses. In the midst of their overtly fictional or 'alternative' worlds, these novels *do* present the reader with 'perfect matches'. They offer not 'general matches' (as realism) but historically determinate particulars. Such novels suggest that history itself is a multiplicity of 'alternative worlds', as fictional as, but other than, the worlds of novels. They suggest this by inserting real historical events or personages into an overtly fictional context.

Discussing the development of narrative, Scholes and Kellogg have argued that the novel emerged as a resynthesis on the one hand of the 'empirical' components of epic (history/mimesis) and on the other hand of its 'fictional' components (romance/fable). They go on to argue that the novel is at present breaking down into its original components but reverting to the purely 'fictional' (Scholes and Kellogg 1966). David Lodge has suggested that 'it would be equally possible to move in the opposite direction – towards empirical narrative and away from fiction' (Lodge, 1977b, p. 90). And certainly 'non-fiction' novels like Truman Capote's *In Cold Blood* (1965), the collection in *The New Journalism* (1973) by Tom Wolfe and E. W. Johnson, or more recently Thomas Keneally's *Schindler's Ark* (1982) remind us that, as one critic has said: 'the longest lasting and most incestuous of the novel's many marriages and affairs has been with journalism' (Raban 1970, p. 71).

Novels like E. L. Doctorow's *The Book of Daniel* (1971) and Robert Coover's *The Public Burning* (1977) are both 'non-fiction' *and* metafictional novels, 'empirical' *and* 'fictional'. Mas'ud Zavarzadeh has, in fact, suggested that both 'non-fiction' and the metafictional novel anyway share 'a radical refusal to neutralize the contingent nature of reality by transforming it into a safe zone of unified meaning' (Zavarzadeh 1976, p. 41). Non-fiction novels suggest that facts are ultimately fictions, and metafictional novels suggest that fictions are facts. In both cases, history is seen as a provisional construct.

Historical writing matches a determinate individual object with a direct representation of a determinate individual object (remaining within Ingarden's terms). Fictional writing matches an imaginatively constructed fictional object with a general class of possibly real objects. Fiction is thus always incomplete, always to be completed by a reader. Fictional characters, for example, are not epistemologically indeterminate in the way of 'real' people (because the words on the page *are* the people in fiction). As part of an imaginary world they are always ontologically indeterminate, always uncertainly awaiting completion.

However, metafictional texts which introduce real people and events expose not only the illusion of verisimilar writing but also that of historical writing itself. The people and events here may 'match' those in the real world, but these people and events are always recontextualized in the act of writing history. Their meanings and identities always change with the shift in context. So history, although ultimately a material reality (a presence), is shown to exist always within 'textual' boundaries. History, to this extent, is also 'fictional', also a set of 'alternative worlds'.

The paradox is explored in Robert Coover's novel *The Public Burning*, which draws, on the one hand, from factual historical sources about the events leading up to the Rosenberg execution and, on the other hand, from the patently unreal fantasy figures of American myth and popular culture. What is revealed, however, is the fictional construction of history. The cold war period, and particularly the days leading up to the all-American entertainment phantasmagoria of the trial itself, is shown in a kaleidoscope of perspectives. The novel alternates between a narrative provided by a Richard Nixon whose consciousness is, anachronistically, clearly shaped in terms of post-Watergate (1973) experience, and sections of manic carnivalistic prose featuring the circus acts of Uncle Sam.

Uncle Sam is a comic-book embodiment of the dominant ideology of American society during the last thirty years – an ideology predominantly constructed out of a paranoid fear of communism, and a total belief in material progress and in the United States as superpower. It is shown in the novel to depend for its success on its linguistic and symbolic embodiment in the idols of popular culture: in John Wayne and Walt Disney, in figures like Ben Franklin, in the American constitution, in the 'objectivity' of its mass media. (Chapter 10 presents a parodistic 'Pilgrimage to the *New York Times*'. The mystical experience of the pilgrims gathered together outside its central offices is, however, that of 'the illusion suffered by mystics throughout the ages: the Spirit, annunciating reality, displaces it, and the tangible world dissolves even as it is being proclaimed' (p. 244). They do not, of course, notice the writing on the subway walls – the Hegelian 'OBJECTIFICATION IS THE PRACTICE OF ALIEN-ATION'.)

This ideology is nowhere present more fully than in Nixon's 'personal' chapters. He is absurd because in his desperation to embody Uncle Sam (who finally and ironically as 'Sam Slick the Yankee Fiddler' proves that Nixon has become 'his boy' at last, by sodomizing him in the last few pages of the novel), in his urge to go down in the history of a superpower as its superman, he becomes no man. He completely loses his 'personality'. His identity merges totally with the all-American ideology until he becomes merely its victim. He thus becomes a figure ripe for media scandal and 'historical' reconstruction when the tide of success turns. Since he is a piece of public property, the public can choose to 'sell' him how and when it wishes. Yet all the characters are similarly victims of this ideology. 'History' is the victim of 'fiction'. Julius Rosenberg is determined to 'destroy all this so-called history, so that history can start again' (p. 243). He is also shown to be the victim of ideology in that he naïvely believes that one individual can oppose its hegemony – its pervasive reinforcement and dominance. He naïvely believes that political power can be invested in individuals, that reason can overcome generalized madness.

E. L. Doctorow's *The Book of Daniel* similarly suggests that history is the ultimate fiction we are all living. It proposes also that our personalities are finally always constructed out of ideology, and that individual heroism and sacrifice in a political cause is therefore ultimately futile. The subject of this novel is also the execution of a couple for supposedly betraying the secret of the atom bomb to the Russians (though this couple, the Isaacsons, are a fictional version of the Rosenbergs). Their 'fictional' story is told, however, within a context of references to historical 'facts'. These include persons such as Norman Mailer, Dr Spock, Bob Taft, Joe McCarthy, Robert Lowell and Richard Burton, and events like the march on the Pentagon. History textbooks are cited (with authentic references) along with sociological analyses of aspects of American culture such as Disneyland.

What emerges again is history as text: history as personal reconstruction. In this novel, however, the 'personal' lives of the fictional characters carry far more of the weight of narrative interest than in *The Public Burning*. The narrative is presented through three levels: the 'story' (*histoire*) of Paul and Rochelle Isaacson, imprisoned for betraying their country, and of their children Daniel and Susan, ending with the Isaacsons' execution; the 'story' (at the level of *discours*) of Daniel and Susan in 1967, beginning with the failure of Susan's attempted suicide but still ending with her funeral; and the 'story' (at the level of *narration* itself) of the progress of the novel we are reading, as Daniel sits composing it in the library of Columbia University, and ending with the ending of the novel.

The level of narration keeps the process of fictional/historical construction continually in the reader's mind. Daniel writes instructions to himself to 'strike that' (p. 24) or to 'explore the history of corporal punishment as a class distinction' (p. 133). He even refers to his professor, Sukenick (who is an actual living writer and critic of metafiction), for whom Daniel seems to be writing the story we are reading. The personal stories, the fictional lives, are shown throughout as constructed by 'history'. Daniel's despair and cynicism about revolutionary protest against Vietnam in the sixties, for example, is shown as a consequence of his childhood history, of the effects of his parents' optimistic, austere and fervent socialist commitment in the fifties.

Yet 'history' is itself shown as a fictional construction. Daniel's 'character' and place in it have been fixed by his parentage. He has no more freedom than a character in a fiction (which, of course, he is). There is, he says, 'nothing I can do, mild or extreme, that they cannot have planned for' (p. 74). He is the son of a traitor and therefore a traitor himself. He cannot escape the fiction that is history or the history that is fiction. He cannot escape at a personal level, through his own wife and child, or at a social level, through his acts in the world, or even at the level of language, as a character in a novel, writing like Holden Caulfield his 'David Copperfield kind of crap' (p. 98). At each narrative level the transformation goes on.

Worlds of words: the 'fantastic' as an alternative world

An interesting version of the 'alternative worlds' view of fiction is that presented in Todorov's work on the fantastic. As with all 'alternative worlds' positions, he begins with the view that 'literary discourse cannot be true or false, it can only be valid in relation to its own premises' (Todorov 1973, p. 10). The essence of the 'fantastic' in his view is that it 'hesitates' both understanding and definition of the 'reality' outside the fiction. All metafictional texts question precisely this 'existence of an irreducible opposition between real and unreal' (ibid., p. 167). Many of them pursue their questioning through the self-conscious construction of alternative worlds which contest the 'reality' of the everyday world, or of each other. Angela Carter's strange and mythically allusive kingdoms, Gilbert Sorrentino's and D. M. Thomas's 'hotels', John Fowles's Bourani, John Hawkes's surrealistic portrait of an occupied Germany (*The Cannibal* (1949), Italo Calvino's invisible cities of Kubla Khan's realm: these are all explicitly 'alternative', broadly 'fantastic'.

Doris Lessing's *The Memoirs of a Survivor* (1974), for example, is not *overtly* metafictional but it does 'hesitate' the distinctions between 'fiction' and 'reality' by setting two alternative worlds against each other. The first, or outer frame, is a futuristic projection of the everyday world, a city recovering from a nuclear holocaust. Set against this is a second, mental world mediated through Jungian symbols and mythic archetypes. The symbol of this world is not a *city* (always in Lessing's work suggesting the alienated contemporary consciousness) but a *room* (again in her novels suggesting the fragile inner psyche). The alternatives are familiar ones in Lessing's fiction. In *The Golden Notebook* Anna's Jungian analyst Mrs Marks tries to persuade her to see her personal past in terms of a Jungian collective unconscious, to heal the divisions within herself by submerging her identity as an individual into that of the archetypal artist-seer. Significantly, Anna identifies Mrs Marks with a room:

> Nothing in my life corresponds with anything in this room – my life has always been crude, unfinished, raw, tentative . . . it occurred to me looking at this room that the raw, unfinished quality in my life was precisely what was valuable in it and I should hold on fast to it.

(p. 239)

Anna feels her world at this particular historical moment to be so radically different from any other, however, that she rejects the possibility of discovering unity in archetypal patterns. Art that expresses such an order is invalidated by contemporary experience. She rejects tradition, for the future may be a completely different reality: 'Terrible, perhaps, or marvellous, but something new' (p. 460).

This vision divides in *The Memoirs of a Survivor* into two possible alternative realities: the city is a development of the 'something new', and the inner world of the room is a development of Mrs Marks's 'old and cyclical'. However, Lessing tries to assert in this novel that a radical, historically materialist break (such as that presented in *The Four-Gated City*) will not save civilization. Hope lies only with the reassertion of the inner psyche through its submergence in the greater mind of the collective unconscious. The narrator gradually withdraws from the outer, city world into the inner world of the rooms behind the wall. She enters a mental world where she journeys back into a personal and collective racial and female past. This inner world finally triumphs over the historical one. It becomes the outer frame, as the narrator, Emily and Hugo walk resolutely towards the wall at the end of the novel, 'Out of this collapsed little world into another order of world altogether' (p. 190).

It has been seen through Berger and Luckmann's work, however, that the everyday world exerts a massive force to resist the attempts of alternative worlds or symbolic systems to become paramount reality. It has been seen through Goffman's work that the outer frame always defines 'reality'. As the novel begins, the reader settles into the basically realistic outer frame of the city world (an extension of the 'everyday'); but he or she is suddenly plunged into a different reality and a different frame (through the wall) where laws of time and space are suspended. Allusions to *Alice in Wonderland*, Freudian oral fantasies and Jungian motifs – the child, the garden, the strange woman – intermingle.

The frames change, but they ignore each other. They even contradict each other. The inner world takes over the superior reality status accorded to the outer frame, but the historical world (now the inner frame) exerts the special claim to paramount status of the 'everyday'. The explicitly symbolic inner world is never integrated with the apparent historical world. The weighty symbolism has no anchorage in any reference to 'literal' objects, either in the city world or in the world of the everyday.

The two worlds question each other throughout. They continue, fantastically, to 'hesitate' each other, even though Lessing tries to resolve this hesitation at the end of the novel by asserting the primacy of the inner world. The validity of this symbolic world has just not been firmly enough established for the reader to abandon his or her historical perspectives. What the novel does powerfully assert, however, is a metafictional affirmation of the inadequacy of a mutually exclusive opposition of the concepts 'reality' and 'fiction'.

John Fowles's *The Magus* (1965, 1977) is another novel which explicitly constructs an 'alternative world' as a metaphor for the processes of fictionality. Bourani provides a classic 'fantastic' setting: 'second meanings hung in the air, ambiguities, unexpectednesses' (p. 85). The protagonist, Nick, arrives there to take up a job. He is immediately drawn into Conchis's (ultimately Fowles's) 'godgame', and responds with the involvement that Todorov sees as essential in securing the reader's identification, and the hesitation that forces him or her to question the ontological status of what is happening. Framed by the humdrum scenes of everyday life in London, Bourani shifts realism to gothic (similar to the structure of Iris Murdoch's *The Unicorn* (1963), David Storey's *Radcliffe* (1963) and Ian McEwan's *The Comfort of Strangers* (1981)). The reader accepts the shift, however, because it is mediated through a character who is not only involved but sceptical too. It is continually indicated that Bourani, like the novel itself and Conchis's masques, is explicitly an art-world, a metaphor. The reader is warned early on of this. Nick, looking back at his inauthentic existence at Oxford, reflects that he misinterpreted 'metaphorical descriptions of complex modes of feeling for straightforward presentation of behaviour' (p. 17). The reader is being warned not to do the same.

Todorov argues further in his work on the fantastic:

If certain events of a book's universe explicitly account for themselves as imaginary, they thereby contest the imaginary nature of the rest of the book. If a certain apparition is only the fault of an overexcited imagination, then everything around it is real.

(Todorov 1973, p. 168)

Although, as Fowles recognizes, the reality of fiction is primarily verbal, the imaginary world generated by the words of a novel is not less real than, but an *alternative* to, the everyday world. *The Magus* is about Nick's attempts to learn to perceive the fictional basis of everything and to distinguish between different orders of fiction.

One way of reinforcing the notion of literary fiction as an alternative world is the use of literary and mythical allusion which reminds the reader of the existence of this world outside everyday time and space, of its thoroughgoing textuality *and* intertextuality. Fowles's character Conchis is explicitly derived from Shakespeare's (Prospero), the tarot's and Jung's (trickster) magus figures. He is a version of the Jungian 'shadow' who seems to be 'hiding meaningful contents under an unprepossessing exterior' (Jung 1972, p. 150). He takes over the telling of the story for much of the central section of the novel and is frequently compared with a novelist creating 'a world where nothing is certain' (*The Magus*, p. 339). He is a novelist like Fowles himself and, like the definition of a god in *The Aristos* (1965), has 'freedom' and 'hazard' as his first principles.

Conchis demonstrates to Nick the need for existential authorship in all human beings, and Nick is made aware of the existence of multiple worlds or 'realities' which cannot be contained between the covers of any book, the score of a symphony or the parameters of a stage. They refuse such closure, because, in Conchis's own words, the curtain never falls and the play always goes on acting. He steers Nick through a Jungian night journey under the sea. Nick, unravelling Conchis's mysteries, is clearly a Theseus figure for much of the novel, but on his return to London, and before he reaches the centre, he becomes an Orpheus bringing back his Eurydice from the dead (Alison's 'suicide').

The Magus sets out to explore the artistic process of constructing novels and lives. Ostentatious use of literary and mythic allusion reinforces the notion of fictionality, and the reader's awareness of the construction of alternative worlds. Such explicit intertextual reminders are common in metafictional novels and suggest to the reader that

> The ongoingness of tradition – of social process – makes a 'finite' province of meaning impossible, for the boundaries of universes of discourse are constantly merging into one another and reemerging as transformed fields of meaning.
>
> (Stewart 1979, p. 48)

The Prospero figure, for example, recalled here explicitly in the figure of Conchis, makes frequent appearances in metafictional novels. He is there, ironically cast, in Muriel Spark's *Not to Disturb* (1971). In the figure of Lister the butler, he busily and effectively organizes chaos, informing those around him: 'we have been such stuff as dreams are all through the night' (p. 85). This novel is about the production of art in a society as degenerate in integrity and coherence as that portrayed in Webster's *The Duchess of Malfi* (to which it constantly alludes). This society, however, has the technological apparatus to enable any enterprising entrepreneur to take over the role of its artistic producer. Its aristocracy shut themselves away in large rooms full of useless miniatures. Their servants are left, in a parody of classic theatrical tradition, to hold the stage. As the capitalist entrepreneurs of the future, however, they take over the whole drama (the novel is arranged in five sections which correspond to the structure of a Jacobean tragedy).

Excelling in the *ad hoc* conversion of apparently fortuitous events (though nothing, of course, is ultimately fortuitous in the Spark world), Lister uses the gadgetry that modern science and affluence has put at his disposal in order to arrange the future (the foretold deaths of the aristocrats) into sensationalist documentary art. Here is a divided, alienated, thoroughly mechanized world: tape recorders and food processors have cut the servants off from their traditional 'modes of production'. In the Klopstock household 'the books are silent' (p. 44), but Victor Passerat's coat, carefully documented on celluloid, 'speaks volumes' (p. 69). Art is produced in the same way as the sliced carrots which stream out of Heloise's food processor.

In this world, artistic virtuosity has become ingenuity and publicity. In an amoral and irreligious world, art is touted – as so often in Spark's novels – as so much 'real estate'. The servants refer to the future as a thing of the past. They exist within a present-tense narrative but discourse in the future tense because they *know* they are a work of art. They are opportunists. Yet, complacent within the world of high-technology production, they are unaware of an ironic authority outside their world creating them. They might produce the 'story' of their lives to sell to the international press, but their lives are Muriel Spark's story. She does, however, allow them success within their world. They are 'successful' according to the norms of a consumerist, technological society which registers the significance of 'art' in terms of cash value. They have realized a lucrative truth expressed by John Berger, comparing art to advertisement:

> Publicity speaks in the future tense and yet the achievement of this future is endlessly deferred. . . . It remains credible because the truthfulness of publicity is judged, not by the real fulfilment of its promises, but by the relevance of its fantasies to those of the spectator-buyer. Its essential application is not to reality, but to daydreams.
>
> (Berger 1978, p. 146)

What the servants do not realize, however, is that, while they are in the process of creating 'publicity', Muriel Spark is in the process of creating *them*, and creating an alternative world which refers not to 'daydreams' but to the 'reality' of the novel as a work of art. What Lister sees as his self-determined predestination is thus revealed to be merely an aspect of literary form. What we see, in our everyday lives, as self-determined predestination is also revealed to be merely an aspect of eternal form. We too, Spark implies, are created by a higher authority.

5

Fictionality and context: from role-playing to language games

This chapter aims to trace the 'sliding scale' of metafictional practices from those novels which still implicitly invoke the context of the everyday world (though questioning its representation as simply a domain of commonsense) through to those novels which shift context so frequently and so radically that the only 'frame' of which the reader is certain is the front and back covers of the book he or she is holding.

It is dangerous, of course, to make simple distinctions between British and American fiction, but many British writers seem to fit comfortably into the first half of the scale and many American writers into the second half. Even a cursory examination, in fact, would reveal the earlier sensitivity of American fiction to the concept of reality as a construct. Other factors have differently affected the development of both fiction and metafiction in the two countries. America in the sixties saw the emergence of a much more influential youth 'counter-culture', with an attendant growth in political and psychological awareness about issues such as race, war, gender and technology. The fictional legacy from the late fifties and early sixties in America was strongly marked by absurdism and black humour (Joseph Heller's *Catch-22* (1961), for example) rather than the anti-modernist, empiricist writing of England (Kingsley Amis, John Braine, C. P. Snow). The consequence of this has been a strong tendency in US writers to respond to the anonymous, frenetic and mechanized society they see around them with fiction that is similarly depersonalized, hyperactive and over- or under-systematized.

Act I: All the world's a stage: role-playing and fictionality as theme

William H. Gass has written that 'we select, we construct, we compose our pasts and hence make fictional characters of ourselves as it seems we must to remain sane' (Gass 1970, p. 128). The examination of fictionality, through the thematic exploration of characters 'playing roles' within fiction, is the most minimal form of metafiction. It is a form that can be 'naturalized' ultimately to fit realist assumptions. It is not concerned with the *linguistic* existence of the fictional text, nor with questions of its ontological status. Such novels tend to present characters who are involved in a duplicitous situation requiring the perpetration of some form of pretence or disguise. These characters usually appear as inauthentic artists. They may be professional artists such as actors, writers or painters. Or they may be artists because they assume roles which destroy their own and others' integrity and existential freedom, through the confusion of 'role' with 'self', or of appearance with reality. Such novels assume there is an *a priori* reality which can to a large extent be taken for granted, but which is flexible enough to accommodate fictional departures from its norms.

Muriel Spark's novel *The Public Image* (1968) follows the career of Annabel, an actress whose life comes to be determined by the publicity image that has been constructed for her, the 'English Tiger Lady'. Eventually, though, she becomes aware of the fiction-making process and decides to step out of the image, to disappear with her baby whose 'existence gave her the sense of being permanently secured to the world' (p. 125). Spark's Jean Brodie, however, becomes enslaved by her own fictional images of herself and in attempting to impose them upon the schoolgirl minds around her (from advice about skin-cleansing to praise of Mussolini) reveals the fascism latent in a misapplied and obsessive mythologization.

An unusual exploration of the theme of fictionality occurs in Brigid Brophy's *Flesh* (1962), where Marcus's diffuse and ineffectual aestheticism is taken in hand by Nancy's self-assertiveness and culinary skills to function as the raw material from which an *objet d'art* can be produced. Marcus *himself* is turned into a Rubens woman in order to be worthy of Nancy. At their first meeting, he has told Nancy his favourite painter is Rubens, and 'he knew that Nancy must be seeing the contrast between Rubens and his admirer' (p. 17). By the end, disgustingly fat, he can inform her: 'I've become a Rubens woman' (p. 123).

More sinister still is John Barth's *The End of the Road* (1958). Jacob Horner is a grammar teacher who lives his life on the principle of the generative possibilities of substitution and combination offered by 'mythotherapy', a form of compulsive role-playing. Another character, Joe Morgan, is a logician who obsessively categorizes experience according to the rules of pure logic. Between them they bring about the death of Joe's wife (Jacob's lover) through, in Jacob's case, an avoidance of real responsibility and, in Joe's, the inflexibility and inhumanity which is the result of distorting experience to fit predetermined categories.

Some metafictional novels present characters who are explicitly artist figures. They may be novelists writing novels, as in Gide's *The Counterfeiters* (1925), Nigel Williams's *My Life Closed Twice* (1977), Bernard Malamud's *The Tenants* (1971), Philip Roth's *The Ghost Writer* (1979), Iain Crichton-Smith's *Goodbye Mr Dixon* (1974) and John Gardner's *Freddy's Book* (1980). Some involve characters who manipulate others explicitly as though they were playwrights or theatrical directors, as in many of Iris Murdoch's novels, in Fowles's *The Collector* (1963), A. S. Byatt's *The Game* (1967) or Martin Amis's *Success* (1978). In *Goodbye Mr Dixon*, for example, the reader is presented with a novelist haunted by the role he has created for his main character, Dixon, who is a projection of his deepest desires and conflicts. The novelist finds himself unable to lead a normal life because he continually measures this 'real' life against the impossible standards set by the character's life. Envy and personal dissatisfaction, in fact, are frequently shown in these novels to lead to obsessive and uncontrolled practices of self-fictionalization. Alternatively, they may lead, as Albert Camus suggests, to the inauthentic fictionalizing of others, because we 'see only the salient points of these lives without taking into account the details of corrosion. Thus we make these lives into works of art' (*The Rebel* 1951, p. 226).

Iris Murdoch has suggested that fictionalization in life occurs because 'people create myths about themselves, are then dominated by the myths. They feel trapped and they elect other people to play roles in their lives. . . . a novelist is revealing secrets of this sort' (Murdoch 1977, p. 138). Certainly this theme is explored in most of her novels. Ironically, however, despite her argument for preserving the contingent opacity of characters, she often reveals an attraction to systems of complete abstract significance, to the 'crystalline', which, as she herself has said, results in 'far too shallow and flimsy an idea of human personality' (Murdoch 1977, p. 23).

Novels like *The Black Prince* (1973) and *A Word Child* (1975) involve professional artists who self-consciously explore such formal problems: Iris Murdoch's own dilemmas. Bradley Pearson (the 'crystalline' novelist set against the 'journalistic' writer Baffin) is the narrator of *The Black Prince*. The novel is framed by an array of mock textual accoutrements, forewords, editorials and postscripts by narrator, editor and dramatis personae, similar to those in Nabokov's *Lolita*. The title of the novel is itself an indication of its self-referential status. As Pearson explains, *Hamlet* is the play in which Shakespeare gave the role of himself to its hero, and in *The Black Prince* Murdoch seems to be exploring the two sides of *her* fictional dilemma through their embodiment in the two writers in the novel, Pearson and Baffin.

Most of her novels, however, are not so explicit in their metafictional situations. In *A Fairly Honourable Defeat* (1970), for example, implicit references to theatre replace overt references to novelists writing novels. Here she explores the complications that arise from the assumption that we are the heroes or heroines of our own life-dramas rather than part of a larger drama in which we are merely walk-on extras. A play within a play within a play is presented: Morgan dresses up as a girl dressed up as a boy, trapped in Julius's flat. Simon and Julius eavesdrop in a manner reminiscent of Jacobean revenge drama. Comic misunderstandings proliferate. Julius is presented as an enchanter/voyeur rather like Iago. Rupert, like Othello, kills himself because of the deception worked upon him and because Julius, at one with the Iago role, cannot comprehend the depth of human passion. The reader is left with a vision, both tragic and comic, essentially absurd, of what happens when people try to fit others into preordained roles in their own dramas, left with 'how very little any of us actually know at any given moment about the consequences of our actions' (p. 433).

Act II: Curtain-up: script-writing

Why do metafictional novelists so frequently concern themselves with the problem of human freedom? Malcolm Bradbury's parody of Muriel Spark and John Fowles in *Who Do You Think You Are?* (1976), for example, focuses precisely on this aspect of their work. Three nuns are walking in a garden (an imitation of the opening scenario of Spark's *The Abbess of Crewe*):

> 'I wish we could get ourselves into the hands of Mr Fowles,' says Sister Mercy as they walk back in their black habits, 'He's much kinder and allows his people an extraordinary freedom of choice.' 'We understand your feelings,' says Sister Georgiana, 'but it's a very secular judgement.'
>
> (p. 173)

For Spark, freedom is limited to self-conscious role-playing because in fiction characters are trapped within the novelist's script, and in 'reality' people are part of the book written by the hand of God. For Fowles too, 'pretending your characters are free can only be a game' (Fowles 1976, p. 456). For him, the author is still a god, but 'what has changed is that we are no longer the Gods of the Victorian image, with freedom our first principle, not authority' (*The French Lieutenant's Woman*, p. 86). The concern with freedom in both cases is, however, a consequence of the perceived analogy between plot in fiction and the 'plot' of God's creation, ideology or fate. It is a concern with the idea of being trapped within someone else's order. At the furthest metafictional extreme, this is to be trapped within language itself, within an arbitrary system of signification which appears to offer no means of escape.

In their sociological work *Escape Attempts*, Stanley Cohen and Laurie Taylor discuss the implications of living within a daily routine which can be compared to the experience of living in a prison. They suggest, however, that any analogy between fictional characters and real people finally breaks down. For 'real' people there are always alternative scripts. The 'script then is simultaneously the launching pad for identity work and a battleground on which to fight for a separate identity' (Cohen and Taylor 1978, p. 68). Fictional characters have no identity *outside* the script, and do not ultimately have identity *within* the script. One common metafictional strategy is to present characters who are aware of this condition, and who thus implicitly draw attention to the fictional creation/description paradox. The characters in Samuel Beckett's *Endgame* (1957) know the script to be a machine, an alternative to destiny, as do Tom Stoppard's Rosencrantz and Guildenstern and Luigi Pirandello's six characters. The device is an obvious theatrical strategy because of the *prima facie* existence of the script in drama. In fiction, characters normally know of their condition through knowledge of their relationship to an author. Denis Potter's novel *Hide and Seek* (1973), for example, begins with its oversexed 'hero', Daniel, trying to explain how his life has been imposed upon by a morally sick author who has imprisoned him in 'This dirty Book' (p. 7).

In most of Spark's novels the author is flaunted as God in the novel, though necessarily a humanly fallible one. This is achieved through the plot device of prematurely revealing the ends of the characters in 'flashforwards' near the beginning of the book. Reading such a novel for the first time, with its exaggerated sense of an ending and technique of advanced significance, is like the second reading of a conventional novel. Causal relationships and perfect systems of order (or almost: this is the closest we can get, in human terms, to the divine plan) are foregrounded. Events immediately take on significances in ways which are impossible in life, where the end cannot be known: in ways, however, which are perfectly possible within a world of art placed always in relation to the context, not of the everyday, but of the eternal and absolute.

Muriel Spark's novel-writing career began shortly after her conversion to Roman Catholicism in 1954, the effect of which, she has said, was 'to give me something to work on as a satirist. The Catholic faith is a norm from which one can depart' (Spark 1961, p. 60). So too is the traditional novel. Acceptance and simultaneous subversion of both her faith and the novel form provide her metafictional base. They facilitate her satirical treatment of the irrationalities of a world where everyone has forgotten God, through the stylized creation of fictional worlds where absolutely no one, and certainly not the reader, is allowed to.

Sometimes her characters know they are being written into a fiction. Caroline in *The Comforters* (1957), listening to the type-writer creating the novel in which she is a character, has her thoughts taken over continually by the thoughts of her author, which are the novel she is in:

> On the whole she did not think there would be any difficulty with Helena.
> Just then she heard the sound of a typewriter. It seemed to come through the wall on her left. It stopped, and was immediately followed by a voice remarking her own thoughts. It said: on the whole she did not think there would be any difficulty with Helena.
>
> (p. 42)

Sometimes the characters believe they are creating their own fictional identity, but the reader always knows that it is being created for them. In *The Driver's Seat* (1970) the present-tense narrative describing Lise in search of a man to murder her suggests that Lise is in control, is creating her own history. It is counterpointed, however, by the analeptic use of the future tense which reveals her 'end' to the reader (and the 'end' of Spark's plot) very near the beginning of the book. As George Steiner has suggested:

> Future tenses are an example of the more general framework of non- and counter-factuality. They are a part of the capacity

of language for the fictional and illustrate absolutely central powers of the human word to go beyond and against 'that which is the case'.

(Steiner 1975, p. 61)

Ironically, their use here reminds the reader that Lise's 'script' exists within a larger 'script' (Spark's) which exists within a final script (God's).

In *The World According to Garp* (1976) John Irving uses an array of similar strategies, but the apparently everyday world in this novel is even more bizarre and surreal than the overtly fictional worlds also presented. The final authority here is only T. S. Garp himself. He is a 'war baby' born of the last act of wounded ball-turret gunner Technical Sergeant Garp, 'an idiot with a one-word vocabulary' (p. 18) – 'Garp!' As in Spark's fiction, the base tense of the novel, the past historic, is continually broken into by forms of the future tense, which act as constant reminders of fictionality. The impersonal narrative version of events uses simple flashforwards itself: 'Jenny's only other brother would be killed in a sailboat accident long after the war was over' (p. 10). This base narrative is counterpointed at intervals by Garp's mother's version – 'In her autobiography Jenny wrote: "I wanted a job and I wanted to live alone. That made me a sexual suspect" ' (p. 13) – and by Garp's version (inserted into the narrative at intervals well before Garp has even been conceived in the order of the plot): ' "My mother," Garp wrote, "was a lone wolf" ' (p. 4).

Jenny Fields, his mother, publishes her autobiography and becomes a feminist *cause célèbre*. Garp, worried at 'becoming a public figure – a leading character in someone else's book before he'd even written a book of his own' (p. 130), decides also to write. The novel contains several of his stories, surreal distillations of the absurd and equally grotesque events of his 'real' life in Irving's novel. Garp's wife, Helen, suggests that his fiction is, in fact, no different from autobiography: 'You have your own terms for what's fiction and what's fact,' she tells him. 'It's all your *experience* – somehow, however much you make up, even if it's only an imagined experience' (p. 162).

This is not surprising, given the bizarre world in which he

lives – the context which, in the novel, is supposed to approximate in its 'realistic' presentation to our own everyday world. Irving reiterates Roth's view of the American writer's relation to 'reality' – there's no outdoing it. The novel, however, also suggests that any history, any autobiography, is always a reconstruction, a fiction. The individual recounting his or her life is a different individual from the one who lived it, in a different world, with a different script. 'Jenny Fields' is fictional not only because she is created by John Irving but because as soon as any of us put ourselves on paper we create fictional characters of ourselves. And as soon as any of us put fictional characters on paper, we write our own autobiographies, the 'scripts' of our lives.

An earlier character who pondered the relationship between fiction and autobiography was Sartre's Roquentin (*Nausea*, 1938). For him, however, there was finally a choice between living and recounting, although a human being will always try to 'live his life as if he were recounting it' (p. 61). In a post-modernist age, however, this no longer seems to be the case, especially in novels, which are about 'characters' before they are about 'human beings'.

John Fowles's *The French Lieutenant's Woman* is interesting in that it attempts to explore an existential concern with human freedom through a writerly awareness that characters in fiction, in predetermined fictional 'scripts', can never really be free. Fowles offers the reader three endings – alternatives to both Victorian morality and historical-romance conventions – but he himself would agree with the critics that life, of course, offers an infinity of possible endings (though he might prefer the term 'history' to 'life'). Like Spark, Fowles is interested in endings as they relate to the problem of freedom, and also in the possible outcome of setting past against present in the sphere of fiction. Spark, however, works through an opposition of present and future verb tenses. Fowles prefers to set centuries – nineteenth and twentieth – against each other and has described the novel as a 'science fiction journey back in time' (Fowles 1969, p. 90).

Like Spark's temporal dislocations, Fowles's too are designed to shake the reader's conventional moral and aesthetic assumptions. At one point, having spent several pages spoofing

Victorian sexual hypocrisy, he shifts the historical context to implicate the reader. Just in case he or she might be settling into a state of passive complacency, he intrudes to comment:

> By transferring to the public imagination what they left to the private, we are the more Victorian – in the derogatory sense of the word – century, since we have in destroying so much of the mystery, the difficulty, the aura of the forbidden, destroyed also a great deal of the pleasure.
>
> (p. 234)

Fowles would be the first to admit that laying bare the conventions does not always increase the pleasure of the text. He suggests (both in the novel and elsewhere) that realism, with its blanks and silences, its repressions, like Victorian sexuality and nineteenth-century history, can also preserve freedom by preserving mystery. Through his manipulation of both realistic convention and Victorian history, he can choose, as author, when to mystify and when to reveal. His characters, clearly, do not have this choice. However, in all of his novels, the characters who deny the possibility of freedom (in existential terms) are those who compulsively label, fix, categorize and define. This is true of the butterfly-collecting Clegg in *The Collector*, as it is of Daniel at the beginning of *Daniel Martin* (1977), who can fix images upon screens but who shuns the area of imaginative freedom allowed by the verbal sign.

In *The French Lieutenant's Woman* Charles Smithson, the dilettante palaeontologist and leisured aristocratic hero, has to be led by Sarah Woodruff, the Victorian social outcast of the title, to a recognition of what freedom entails: 'Escape is not one act . . . each minute the nail waits to be hammered in' (p. 284). Each minute requires a fresh choice, a new direction. He also learns that only thus will history cease to be 'always this being caught in the same fiendish machine' (p. 179). The lesson, however, will be a difficult one, given an author who often treats him as 'a poor living fossil' (p. 257), an author who reveals him to be apparently trapped within both the script of history and the script of the fiction we are reading.

Fowles's novel rehearses George Eliot in its intrusive moralizing. It rehearses Dickens in its portrayal of characters like

Charles's manservant Sam. Arnold is rehearsed through its suggestion of a suspension between two worlds, Hardy in its mysterious heroine. Quotes from Marx, Linnaeus and Darwin provide a subtext for the drama. But always the rehearsal is under the direction of a Roland Barthes, or a French New Novelist, or even a Harold Robbins – suggesting that only if one is self-consciously aware that 'history' like 'fiction' is provisional, continually reconstructed and open-ended can one make responsible choices within it and achieve a measure of freedom.

The novel illustrates John Barth's comment that 'if Beethoven's sixth were composed today, it would be an embarrassment; but clearly, it wouldn't be, necessarily, if done with ironic intent by a composer quite aware of where we've been and where we are' (Barth 1977, p. 75). The important thing is to *admit* one's authorship, *admit* the provisionality of one's constructions. Fowles has to admit that his characters cannot be 'free' because they are written into his script. Yet he has also to admit that they are 'free' to be reconstructed in other people's imaginations, and even in other people's (film) scripts. He may, as a twentieth-century 'Manager of the Performance', confidently and flamboyantly display in an array of epigraphs and documentary footage his knowledge of the Victorians. He may demonstrate that he knows them in ways that they could not possibly know themselves. But if they are in his 'script' he is also in theirs. He can know them only from his own twentieth-century perspective, his own version of history, which can recount their lives but not live them. The epigraphs offer a commentary on the age from within its own perspective; the narrator has only hindsight and the epigraphs to rely upon for his.

The exploration of history and freedom is focused through the characterization of Sarah. She is, even in her introduction, presented more like 'a figure from myth, than any proper fragment of the petty provincial day' (p. 9). Within the world of the fiction, and as a creation of John Fowles, it is Sarah who carries the responsibility for demonstrating most thoroughly Fowles's philosophy of freedom and fiction. She is 'mythical': she stands outside 'history' and outside fiction. She haunts Fowles in his 'real' life. But she achieves this condition in the novel through deliberate artifice. Sarah constructs a fictional version of her life (that she is a 'fallen woman') in order to stand outside conventional Victorian society in the role of social outcast (just as Fowles seeks fictional freedom by standing outside, and exploiting, the fictional conventions of Victorian realism).

Like Conchis, Sarah is a trickster figure, deliberately deceiving, confusing, seducing, using fictional wiles to avoid existential bad faith, existing necessarily in a state of 'alienation'. Fowles ensures that *his* narrative presentation reinforces *her* mysteriousness. The reader is given no access to Sarah's thoughts. The narrator never allows her perspective or voice to be heard through his own. He admits that she haunts him, that she is possibly an aspect of his psychic creativity, his anima. Yet it is in the presentation of Sarah that Fowles, perhaps unintentionally, violates his own principles of freedom.

In fact, both women in the novel – Sarah and Ernestina – conform to stereotypical *male* images of women. If Ernestina is the little angel in the house, Sarah is the *femme fatale*: seductive, treacherous, mysterious and unpredictable. And, paradoxically, this detracts from her 'mystery'. She is not free because contained within and constructed through the patriarchal ideology embodied most powerfully in the narrator himself. He can resist the crude labels of 'hysteric' or 'fallen woman' but not the more subtle implications of virginity combined with predatoriness.

Simone de Beauvoir has argued that, 'Now feared by the male, now desired or even demanded, the virgin would seem to represent the most consummate form of the feminine mystery; she is therefore its most disturbing and at the same time its most fascinating aspect' (Beauvoir 1979, p. 184). Fowles creates a heroine who determines the course of most of the novel (and its possible interpretations) through her *apparently* lost virginity, her label 'whore'. Then, almost at the end, he determines a re-reading of that novel by revealing her decision to deceive society into believing that she is a 'fallen woman' while actually never having lost that virginity which it values so highly. Fowles, then, creates a heroine who at one and the same time fulfils *contradictory* male desires, is both apparent seductress and in fact virgin. She is a heroine who thus ultimately conforms to a male concept of female *contradictoriness* embodied in the *femme fatale* figure. Nineteenth-century 'mystery' in this context merges with twentieth-century oppression, but it is perhaps unfair to expect Fowles to know that perhaps *these* are 'the shadows' out of which Sarah comes (p. 84).

Fowles's notion of fictional 'possession' in relation to fictional freedom is often treated much more literally in metafictional novels. In Clarence Major's *Reflex and Bone Structure* (1975) the author is one of the lovers of the central character Cora Hull, a Greenwich Village actress. He is in love with her, however, *explicitly* as a verbal construction. He lingers seductively, not over her body or the clothes she wears, but over the sound of the words which *are* her body and *are* her clothes.

Flann O'Brien's *At Swim-Two-Birds* is about a writer called Trellis whose characters assert their autonomous identities and devise rebellious plots against him while he is asleep and therefore not in 'possession' of them. Fowles suggested of Sarah that she 'haunted' him; in this novel the characters much more literally possess their author when he is unconscious, just as he, tyrannically, possesses them when conscious. Borges has, of course, discussed the effect of such novels in his essay, 'Partial Magic in the Quixote':

> Why does it disturb us that Don Quixote be a reader of the *Quixote* and Hamlet a spectator of *Hamlet*? I believe I have found the reason: these inversions suggest that if the characters of a fictional work can be readers or spectators, we, its readers or spectators, can be fictitious. In 1833, Carlyle observed that the history of the universe is an infinite sacred book that all men write and read and try to understand, and in which they are also written.
>
> (*Labyrinths*, p. 231)

An interesting version of this is presented in Kurt Vonnegut's *Slaughterhouse-Five*. The 'real' world (how Vonnegut comes to write a book about the fire-bombing of Dresden) is here set against a fictional world (the bombing seen through the eyes of Billy Pilgrim, later an optometrist who prescribes 'corrective lenses for Earthling souls'; p. 26) and an ultra-fictional world with which Billy communicates, the planet Tralfamadore. The latter, however, is explicitly an art-world. Its artificial form and philosophical beliefs are echoed in the form of the novel we are reading with its overtly spatial structure, its circular songs, its repetitious phrases like 'So it goes'.

The motif of script-writing is implied here in the exploration of the relationship of moral and aesthetic responsibility, the relationship of fictions like the one we are reading ('fantasies') to atrocities like the Dresden fire-bombing. Tralfamadore offers Billy an escapist 'Imaginative Space' from which he can view human atrocity with equanimity, but, if 'there is nothing intelligent to say about a massacre', why not escape? Realism, it is suggested, 'isn't enough anymore', realism presents characters, but

> There are almost no characters in this story and almost no dramatic confrontations, because most of the people in it are so sick and so much the listless playthings of enormous forces. One of the main effects of war, after all, is that people are discouraged from being characters.
>
> (p. 110)

Realism presents history as linear chronology, presents characters in the terms of liberal humanism, allows for the possibility of free will and responsible moral choice. But the novel implies that events like Dresden invalidate such liberal assumptions. They are revealed to be inadequate fictions which are possibly as much evasions of responsibility as the construction of Tralfamadorian kingdoms.

Tralfamadore is, in fact, explicitly an aesthetic fantasy world premised upon a rejection of the philosophical and aesthetic assumptions underpinning realism. It is a Symbolist world. Its own art is created to reveal that art cannot change the world because the world, like art, is fixed for ever. Art should aim simply at creating

> an image of life that is beautiful and surprising and deep. There is no beginning, no middle, no end, no suspense, no moral, no causes, no effects. What we love in our books are the depths of many marvellous moments seen all at one time.
>
> (pp. 62–3)

The Tralfamadorians look with some amusement upon the Earthling world of history (and realism) because, from their perspective within a frozen aesthetic eternity, the script is fixed: 'all moments, past, present and future, always have existed, always will' (p. 25). There is no freedom, and therefore no anxiety. Darwin is for them the most engaging human figure, teaching 'that those who die are meant to die, that corpses are improvements' (p. 140). Human schemes of progression are seen to be based on a fundamental stasis: life occurs so that death occurs so that life occurs. 'So it goes.'

Within the perspectives of Tralfamadore, therefore, Billy ceases to feel pain. He need no longer despair or protest or resist, for 'everything was beautiful and nothing hurt' (p. 84). But Vonnegut is *not* Billy. Certainly *Slaughterhouse-Five* suggests that realism is an inadequate means of portraying experiences like Dresden. Vonnegut even breaks the frame of the Dresden section by appearing in it himself – 'an old fart with his memories and his pall malls' (p. 9). However, he cannot (nor does his novel) embrace an aesthetic that ignores the responsibility of literary fiction to engage with history, with the temporal world.

Slaughterhouse-Five is more 'real' than Tralfamadore, even within the covers of *Slaughterhouse-Five*. Vonnegut's 'historical' world stands in relation to Tralfamadore as Nabokov's Antiterra (another self-conscious artistic world) stands in relation to Terra (a world of atrocity clearly analogous to our own historical world) in the novel *Ada* (1969). Both novels reject realism *and* extreme fabulation. They suggest that the construction of alternative worlds should not be an activity that ignores the events and logic of the historical world but should provide an unfamiliar perspective on that world. Thus, if novels cannot *prevent* disasters like Dresden, they can at least change people's attitudes to them. If the novelist does not assume some such responsibility, then (as the discussion at the end of *Slaughterhouse-Five* suggests) the function of the novel will, indeed, become one of providing 'touches of colour in rooms with all-white walls' or of describing 'blow-jobs artistically' (p. 137). It is not at all certain that Vonnegut does not believe this to be already the case. But he does continue to write.

'So it goes.' Of course.

Act III: Some characters in search of an author

Until this point on our necessarily somewhat arbitrary scale, metafiction maintains a finely balanced tension between awareness of its literary-fictional condition and its desire to create imaginative realities, alternative worlds, in which the reader can still become absorbed. From here on, however, texts slip further and further away from the construction of worlds whose 'meaning' is finally dependent on reference to everyday contexts. They slide more and more towards the pure assertion of not only their own linguistic condition but also that of this 'everyday world'.

A last, desperate strategy before the game is handed over entirely to language is to admit that one is telling a story, creating an alternative world. Such an admission functions, however, merely to assert more emphatically that 'one' exists, 'one' is the source of this world, 'one' is an author. However, once 'one' is recognized as itself a construction produced through textual relationships, then worlds, texts and authors are subsumed by language. From this point, the tension breaks down, the balance between the construction of realistic illusion and its deconstruction gives way; the metafictional tension of technique and counter-technique is dissolved, and metafictional elements are superseded by those of surrealism, the grotesque, randomness, cut-ups and fold-ins.

For some metafictional novelists, an alternative to rejecting a simplistic concept of *mimesis* (the belief that verbal constructions can somehow directly imitate non-verbal ones) is to assert the opposite narrative pole of *diegesis*: 'telling' instead of 'showing'. All metafiction draws attention to the fact that imitation in the novel is not the imitation of existing objects but the fabrication of fictional objects which could exist, but do not. For some writers, however, the text may be a fictional construction, but the author is not. All else may be ontologically insecure and uncertain, but behind the uncertainty is a lone Creative Figure busily inventing and constructing, producing the text from His (*sic*) position in the Real World. And the text, it is usually asserted, is finally the author's:

I want my ideas to be expressed so precisely that the very minimum of room for interpretation is left. Indeed I would go further and say that to the extent that a reader can impose his own imagination on my words, then that piece of writing is a failure. I want him to see my (vision) . . .

(B. S. Johnson, *Aren't You Rather Young to be Writing Your Memoirs?*, p. 28)

While modernism pursued impersonality ('showing'), such contemporary metafictional texts pursue Personality, the ironic flaunting of the Teller. They reveal, in Genette's words, that, ' "montrer", ce ne peut être qu'une façon de raconter' (Genette 1972, p. 187). The *appearance* of mimesis, of 'showing', is produced, however, by constructing an ostensibly autonomous reality through maximum information and minimum narratorial presence. Metafictional novels which hang on to the concept of author as inventor of the text, which aim to show there are only 'degrés de diegesis' ('degrees of telling'; Genette 1972, p. 186), exaggerate authorial presence in relation to story or information. Very often the Real Author steps into the fictional world, crosses the ontological divide. Instead of integrating the 'fictional' with the 'real' as in traditional omniscient narrative, he or she splits them apart by commenting not on the *content* of the story but on the act of narration itself, on the *construction* of the story.

Vonnegut's appearances in *Slaughterhouse-Five* have already been mentioned. In *Breakfast of Champions* (1973) his character Kilgore Trout (a trans-textual being who turns up frequently in Vonnegut's fictions) refers to a 'body bag': 'It was a new Invention. . . . I do not know who invented the body bag. I do know who invented Kilgore Trout. I did' (p. 39). Malcolm Bradbury scuttles, in the manner of Hitchcock, across a corridor at Watermouth University in *The History Man*. John Barth corresponds with his characters in *Letters*. He explains as 'J.B.' his role along with the computer WESAC in producing the novel *Giles Goat-Boy* (1966) in the first few pages of the novel. B. S. Johnson foregrounds autobiographical 'facts', reminding the reader in *Trawl* (1966): 'I . . . always with I . . . one starts from . . . one and I share the same character' (p. 9). Or, in *See the Old Lady Decently*, he breaks off a description in the story and informs the reader: 'I have just broken off to pacify my daughter . . . my father thinks she is the image of my mother, my daughter' (p. 27). Steve Katz worries in *The Exaggerations of Peter Prince* (1968) – among *many* other things – about the fact that he is writing the novel under fluorescent light, and wonders how even *this* aspect of the contemporary technological world will affect its literary products.

Alternatively, novelists may introduce friends or fellow writers into their work. Thus, irreverently, in Ronald Sukenick's *98.6* (1975) the 'hero' decides to seduce a girl and her roommate: 'Besides the roommate is a girl who claims to be the lover of Richard Brautigan maybe she knows something. . . . I mean here is a girl saturated with Richard Brautigan's sperm' (p. 26). Federman, Sukenick, Katz and Doctorow make appearances in each others' novels. Steve Katz, in fact, appeared in Ronald Sukenick's novel *Up* (1968) *before* his own first novel, *The Exaggerations of Peter Prince*, had been published (in which Sukenick, of course, in turn appears). Vladimir Nabokov playfully introduces himself into his novels very often through anagrams of variations on his name: Vivian Badlock, Vivian Bloodmark, Vivian Darkbloom, Adam von Librikov (VVN is a pun on the author's initials).

Occasionally authors may wish to remind the reader of their powers of invention for fear that readers may assume fictional information to be disguised autobiography. Raymond Federman writes:

> I have a feeling that if I go
> on giving specific details like these eventually
> they'll think I am talking about myself all the time
> whereas
> in fact
> this is not so   I insist on this point
>   I am inventing most of this
>   (*Double or Nothing*, p. 114)

In fact, third-person narrative with overt first-person intrusion allows for metafictional dislocation much more obviously than first-person narratives (whether the intruding 'I' is the 'real' author or not). In first-person narration the 'telling' is realistically motivated because produced by a personalized figure who is given a spatio-temporal dimension within the fictional world. In third-person/first-person intrusion narratives (such as *Slaughterhouse-Five* and *The French Lieutenant's Woman*), an apparently autonomous world is suddenly broken into by a narrator, often 'The Author', who comes explicitly from an ontologically differentiated world.

The author attempts desperately to hang on to his or her 'real' identity as creator of the text we are reading. What happens, however, when he or she enters it is that his or her own reality is also called into question. The 'author' discovers that the language of the text produces him or her as much as he or she produces the language of the text. The reader is made aware that, paradoxically, the 'author' is situated in the text at the very point where 'he' asserts 'his' identity outside it. As Jacques Ehrmann argues, 'The "author" and the "text" are thus caught in a movement in which they do not remain distinct (the author and the work; one creator of the other) but rather are transposed and become interchangeable, creating and annulling one another' (Ehrmann 1971, p. 32).

Certainly many metafictional writers are themselves aware of, and flaunt, this paradox. Christine Brooke-Rose's *Thru* (1975) ends with an index of 'authors' and sources, beginning (logically?) with Adam, and ending with Yorick, poor. Gilbert Sorrentino points out in *Splendide-Hotel* (1973): 'One wishes simply to say that the writer cannot escape the words of his story, he cannot escape into an idea at all' (p. 13). Perhaps the definitive statement of the paradox is in Borges' *Labyrinths*. 'Borges' and 'I' have a hostile relationship:

> I live, let myself go on living, so that Borges may contrive his literature, and this literature justifies me. It is no effort for me to confess that he has achieved some valid pages, but those pages cannot save me, perhaps because what is good belongs to no one, not even to him, but rather to the language and to tradition.
>
> ('Borges and I', in *Labyrinths*, p. 282)

Roland Barthes has made familiar the concept of 'the death of the author'. It is a paradoxical concept, as metafiction shows.

The more the author appears, the less he or she exists. The more the author flaunts his or her *presence* in the novel, the more noticeable is his or her *absence* outside it. Calvino's *If on a Winter's Night a Traveller* is a fictional completion of Barthes's statement: that the *death* of the author makes possible the *birth* of the reader (Barthes 1977b, pp. 142–9). It is suggested that the narrator, the traveller, is an 'I' who is possibly the 'I' of the author addressing his readers ('by the very fact of writing "I" the author feels driven to put into this "I" a bit of himself'; *If on a Winter's Night a Traveller*, p. 15). He is also an 'I' who talks to the characters *in* the novel, and therefore exists at the level of story *and* at the level of discourse. Finally, as an 'I', he becomes part of the reader's own subjectivity ('because I am called "I" . . . this alone is reason enough for you to invest a part of yourself in the stranger "I" '; p. 15).

By breaking the conventions that separate authors from implied authors from narrators from implied readers from readers, the novel reminds us (who are 'we'?) that 'authors' do not simply 'invent' novels. 'Authors' work through linguistic, artistic and cultural conventions. They are themselves 'invented' by readers who are 'authors' working through linguistic, artistic and cultural conventions, and so on.

There are an increasing number of metafictional novels which similarly play with the relations between story and discourse. A common strategy is to begin a novel in the first person and then to shift to third-person narration and then back again. The first person, 'I', is a member of a grammatical category of words referred to as 'shifters' or 'indexical deictics' – words that can be defined or situated only in relation to their immediate linguistic context or discourse.[10] 'I' is always at the same time both a universal category and a specific speaker defined in relation to a specific speech event. In most first-person narratives (*Jane Eyre*, *Great Expectations*) the *narrating* subject is non-problematically at one with the *narrated* subject (Jane Eyre, woman, recounting her experiences as Jane Eyre, child), both situated in the fictional world created through the speaker's discourse.

Metafictional novels which shift from the personal form 'I' of *discourse* to the impersonal 'he' of *story* remind the reader that the narrating 'I' is the subject of the *discourse*, and is a different 'I' from the 'I' who is the subject of the *story*. And finally, of course, there is yet another level of subjectivity, for behind the whole discourse is the *authorial* 'I', a subjectivity (as the examples in this section have shown) present only in terms of its real absence. Barthes's *Roland Barthes by Roland Barthes* (1977), his autobiography-as-fiction or fiction-as-autobiography, continually draws attention to this paradox:

> I do not say 'I am going to describe myself', but 'I am writing a text and I call it R.B.'. . . . I myself am my own symbol. I am the story which happens to me: freewheeling in language, I have nothing to compare myself to; and in this movement, the pronoun of the imaginary 'I' is *im-pertinent*; the symbolic becomes literally *immediate*: essential danger for the life of the subject: to write oneself may seem a pretentious idea; but it is also a simple idea: simple as the idea of suicide.
>
> (Barthes 1977a, p. 56)

To write of 'I' is to discover that the attempt to fix subjectivity in writing erases that subjectivity, constructs a new subject. The insight is not entirely post-modernist, however. Tristram Shandy desperately attempts to dissolve past, present and future 'selves' into the moment of discourse, the 'now' of his act of narration. He discovers, in the words of the twentieth-century phenomenologist Merleau-Ponty, 'I am never at one with myself' (Merleau-Ponty, 1962, p. 347). And 'I' never will be. To write about onself is implicitly to posit oneself as an 'other', to narrate or historicize oneself as a character in one's own discourse.

Saul Bellow's *Herzog* (1964), Ann Quin's *Passages* (1969), Jerzy Kosinski's *The Devil Tree* (1973), John Irving's *The Water-Method Man* (1972), though not overtly metafictional, all explore this process through shifts of grammatical person. John Fowles's *Daniel Martin* uses the shift between the discursive 'I' and the historic 'he' to explore his favourite theme of existential authorship. He uses the pronominal shifts to reject the modernist premise that consciousness (the certainty that 'I' exist for 'myself') defines existence. He sets out to show that individuals not only construct their own positions in the world and narrate their own histories; they are also situated within others' discourses, are characters in others' fictions.

The novel shows Daniel's attempt to realize authentically his condition of subjectivity. He has to learn that his fictional versions of himself and of others are being used to avoid moral and aesthetic responsibility in the present. This finally entails the recognition that others may indeed possess one in ways that one may not possess oneself. He comes to realize:

> I was writing myself, making myself the chief character in a play so that I was not only the written personage, the character and its actor, but also the person who sits in the back of the stalls admiring what he has written.
>
> (p. 80)

Fowles extends the motif of script-writing along a new axis of grammatical/phenomenological awareness (though not without a large measure of self-indulgence and occasional pretentiousness on the way). Daniel comes to recognize his inauthenticity in terms of the relationship of himself as character (as a third person) to the fictional discourse of his own self as narrator (as first-person 'author' of himself). The reader is also continually made aware that Daniel exists in the fictional discourse of Fowles, 'an I in the hands of fate . . . a paper person in someone else's script' (p. 72). The novel thus becomes the story of writing as much as it is the writing of story.

Act IV: Notes towards the definition of radical metafiction

Metafictional novels at this end of the scale have abandoned 'role-playing' (even the fiction that they are a Fiction, very often) and have embraced a Wittgensteinian concept of 'language games'. They function through forms of radical decontextualization. They deny the reader access to a centre of orientation such as a narrator or point of view, or a stable tension between 'fiction', 'dream', 'reality', 'vision', 'hallucination', 'truth', 'lies', etc. Naturalized or totalizing interpretation becomes impossible. The logic of the everyday world is replaced by forms of contradiction and discontinuity, radical shifts of context which suggest that 'reality' as well as 'fiction' is merely one more game with words.

In an excellent survey of post-modernist fiction, David Lodge (1977, pp. 220–46) has categorized it in terms of contradiction, permutation, discontinuity, randomness, excess, short circuit. Metafiction particularly draws on contradiction, permutation and short circuit. The rest of this chapter will attempt (very briefly) to organize 'radically' metafictional strategies into categories of

CONTRADICTION : PARADOX
OBJETS TROUVÉS : INTERTEXTUAL OVERKILL

All of these strategies depend upon a *tension of opposition* (rather than, say, excess or randomness) which most significantly distinguishes metafiction from other forms of post-modernist fictional writing.

Contradiction

In realist or modernist writing, textual contradictions are always finally resolved, either at the level of plot (realism) or at the level of point of view or 'consciousness' (modernism). In metafictional texts that employ contradiction, there can be no final certainty (no FINAL CURTAIN either), only a reworking of the Liar Paradox, which might run something like this: ' "All novelists are liars," said the metafictionist, truthfully.'

Contradiction implies simultanaeity. Stories like Coover's 'The Babysitter' (*Pricksongs and Descants*) and Barthelme's 'Views of my Father Weeping' (in *City Life*) take the modernist concept of spatial form to a logical conclusion. They offer a set of alternative stories as one story, which can be explained neither as happening *simultaneously* (because they can only be substitutions for each other) nor as happening *in sequence* (because they cannot be combined according to normal logic: they erase or cancel out each other).

Jorge Luis Borges 'The Garden of Forking Paths' (in *Labyrinths*) is both a discussion and an example of such fiction. It is a story of a maze which is a maze of a story. A fourth dimension is posited where numerous possibilities of time and space coexist:

'in some you exist and not I: in others I and not you: in others both of us' (p. 53). The theory is made explicit in the story: 'in all fictional works, each time a man is confronted with several alternatives, he chooses one and eliminates the others: in the fictions of Ts'ui Pên, he chooses – simultaneously – all of them' (p. 51). Readers of the French New Novel will immediately recognize the form this strategy takes in the novels of Alain Robbe-Grillet, for example. The obsessive repetition of incidents within new contexts, slightly shifted, mutually contradictory, occurs throughout *The Voyeur* (1955) or *In the Labyrinth* (1959). These

> always seem to be challenging themselves, casting doubt on themselves all the time they are being constructed. Space destroys time in them, and time sabotages space. Description marks time, contradicts itself, goes round in circles. The moment repudiates all continuity.
>
> (Robbe-Grillet 1965, p. 151)

Robert Coover's stories present similar problems. 'The Baby-sitter' (1971) is divided into 108 sections. Each section forms a narrative unit (narreme) but none of them – read *consecutively* (i.e. with the causal logic of realism) or even *spatially* (i.e. with the associative logic of modernism) – combines to form a unified non-contradictory story. The reader may begin by attempting to construct a causal plot. The scene is set with the babysitter installed with the children. The parents have departed (though not before Mr Tucker's eyes have lustfully lingered over the girl). The babysitter's boyfriend is then seen wandering round pinball-machine arcades debating whether to attempt a first adolescent seduction while the adults are safely at their party.

The outlines of a thriller, a detective story, a romance, a tale of middle-class American domestic life? The opening offers a variety of possibilities for narrative development. The story, however, chooses *all* of them. Nor can the reader naturalize the contradictory alternatives through a modernist reading in terms of shifts of consciousness, or epistemological shifts, say, from 'reality' to dream. The story makes no indication of a difference in 'reality' status of the various sections; it can only be the 'reality' of itself. The 'plots' of many possible 'stories' (including those offered by the television films the babysitter watches) cut across each other in a kaleidoscopic display of arbitrary invention.

The story is possibly a gentle and ironic tale of adolescent sexuality including oedipal and castration complexes. It may be about the decline of a middle-class American marriage. It is perhaps a horrifying story of a sadistic young child-murderer. What about a savage tale of teenage lust? Or the obsessional fantasy life of a latter-day Humbert Humbert? The story is *all* of these stories. It ends with Mrs Tucker's reception of the news that her children are murdered, her husband gone, a corpse in the bath and the house wrecked (surely this one ends with just a little too much overkill?). 'Hell, I don't know,' she says, 'let's see what's on the late night movie' (p. 193). Probably a tale of a babysitter installed with the children, the parents departed (though not before . . .).

In 'The Magic Poker' (1971) Coover uses similarly contradictory series. In this story, however, there is also a very intrusive author who keeps up a continuous commentary on his own ingenuity: 'I wander the island, inventing it. I make a sun for it, and trees' (p. 14). He invents, of course, the poker: the fairy-tale Magic Poker; the Freudian Poker; the Poker which can vandalize and destroy the story; the rusty bit of old iron; the Poker which is the reader reading this story, 'bedded deeply in the bluegreen grass' (p. 31). The poker, like the story and the imagination of its inventor, exists through its power to transform, but exists only as its own transformations. Literal dissolves into metaphorical into allegorical into the words of the story flaunted *as* the words of the story. Karen notices the pubic hair of the suave young man who magically appears when she kisses the poker (which poker?). It fans out like the wings of a wild goose. A wild goose flies out of an old piano. The man laughs at the end and a 'wild goose taste' is left in his mouth (p. 34). The reader seeking to construct an interpretation has also been taken on a very 'wild goose taste'.

Contradiction is the basis for many of the metafictional strategies already discussed in different contexts here. Novels like *Slaughterhouse-Five*, Borges' 'Tlön Uqbar' or Nabokov's *Ada* present mutually contradictory 'worlds'. Beckett's *Watt*,

Nabokov's *Pale Fire* and Murdoch's *The Black Prince* set up contradictions between text and textual accoutrements or footnotes. When such contradictions cannot be resolved (in *The Black Prince*, for example, they can be), such strategies are similarly radical. Alternative endings present another type of contradiction. Fowles's *The French Lieutenant's Woman* has already been mentioned. Brautigan's *A Confederate General from Big Sur* (1964) offers five endings and then suggests 'this book is having 186,000 endings per second' (p. 116). B. S. Johnson's 'Aren't You Rather Young to be Writing your Memoirs?' offers the ending its author had hoped for. The story then contradicts such questionable finality by suggesting that the reader might simply supply his or her own. Johnson, the text asserts, is not in the business of tidying up life; after all, 'Do you ask of your bookmaker that he will explain?' (p. 41). This 'bookmaker' certainly will not.

Contradiction may occur at micro- as opposed to macro-structural levels, within paragraphs, sentences or even phrases. In effect, this results in the incorporation of the principles of surrealism into metafiction: Lautréamont's 'fortuitous meeting on a dissection table, of a sewing machine and an umbrella' (quoted in Stewart 1974, p. 159). Metafiction, however, is more interested in the juxtaposition of contradictory words and phrases which foreground processes of linguistic selection, rather than the surrealistic juxtaposition of extremely disparate images and objects. In Alan Burns's *Celebrations* (1967), for example, a burial is described entirely in terms normally associated with vitality. Synechdoche and metaphor often take on literal status. At an inquest, 'the judges retired to consider their verdict. The two drank the thin white wine, the green and tasty stomachs stood on the polished table . . . each had a slit for dropping in pieces of pie' (p. 26).

Such strategies disorientate the reader by offering no indication of the literal or figurative status of descriptions. Brautigan's *Trout Fishing in America* is entirely constructed through the strategy of metaphorical substitutions taking an apparently literal status in the story. Sometimes writers take a figurative cliché and de-automatize it through a translation into literal terms. The idea of raining cats and dogs becomes a literal reality (it seems) in Barthelme's story 'The Falling Dog' (in *City Life*), where a dog falls from the heavens. In the title story of Barthelme's *Great Days* (1979) we are told of a guy who 'wore his stomach on his sleeve' (p. 161). In Steve Katz's story 'Parcel of Wrists' (1973) a box of human wrists is received through the post, which, when planted, start to produce fruit: eyes, lips, limbs, a crop of legs. In Barthelme's *Snow White*, Jane's mother watches an 'apelike hand' appear through the mailbox. Like the reader she wants to interpret it metaphorically, symbolically. It must mean something. It must stand for something else. But no, says Jane, 'It's just an ape that's all . . . it doesn't mean more than that . . . leave things alone. It means what it means' (p. 107).

The confusion of literal and allegorical worlds is another strategy which offers the reader irresolvable contradictions. In *Darkness Visible* (1979) does Golding's Matty exist 'really' as a strange child who walks out of a bombed city? Is he really a twentieth-century reincarnation of Ezekiel? Or is he an allegorical clarification of the ambiguities of good and evil which are explored through the apparently more 'realistic' characters in the novel, the characters from books 'full of words, physical reduplication of that endless cackle of men' (p. 47)? (Characters who exist, Matty reminds us, only through the endless duplicities of language.) Günter Grass's *The Tin Drum* (1959) offers a similar resistence to total interpretation. Is Oskar, the stunted childlike narrator, a 'real' midget, driven by feelings of spite, lust, rage and destructiveness, or is he an allegorical reflection, in an otherwise realistic fiction, of the anarchic, destructive, libidinous infantilism of Danzig society as it partakes in the rise of Nazism?

Paradox

A paradox is a form of contradiction. It makes an assertion at the moment that it denies that assertion (and vice versa). It offers a finite statement which only infinity can resolve. Such paradoxes of infinity involve the possibility of endless repetition or circularity. These fictional embodiments of 'There was an old man called Michael Finnegan . . .' appear in novels like

Cortázar's *Hopscotch* and *62: A Model Kit* (1972) and Barth's *Letters*, where the novel returns again and again to its (apparent) beginning.

Borges' library of Babel is such a fictional world. So are novels like Robbe-Grillet's *The Erasers* (1953), with its hero a detective who becomes the murderer he has been seeking (apparently). Such fictions again resist resolution within the terms of everyday logic, contexts of 'common sense'. The title of Anthony Burgess's *Abba Abba* (1977) both palindromically suggests such circularity and also, of course, further reinforces the image of linguistic imprisonment in its implicit reference to Keats's pattern of versification. Images of infinite regression remind the reader of the fictive nature of the chronology assumed by realism. One such image is Tristram Shandy's impossible problem of compound interest as he writes his autobiography and realizes that, if he has to write upon his life as he writes, he will never finish. Another is Beckett's exhaustive description of Watt taking a step forward. Watt himself, of course, begins to speak in reverse order. First, words in a sentence, and then letters in a word, then sentences in a period . . . and so on, with infinite variations.

The authors who step into their fictions (discussed in the last section) are locked into a system of endless regress. Their identity disappears the moment that it appears in the fictional text. Barthelme's story 'Sentence' (*City Life*) sets out to be a sentence, to show what a sentence can do. It shows how a sentence can be a clause within a clause within a clause which has at its centre a story, 'The Fantastic Orange Tree', composed of sentences which . . . In another story, the narrator climbs to the top of a glass mountain whose pinnacle is not just a symbol but the symbol of a symbol which disappears at the moment of identification and turns into 'a beautiful princess' (Barthelme, 'The Glass Mountain', *City Life*, pp. 64–5).

The device of the tale within the tale, the nesting of narrators, is another means of suggesting infinite circularity. The potentially endless nesting of quotation marks in Barth's *Chimera* is one of the most overt recognitions of this. However, such images (doublings, mirrorings, nestings, circlings) have to be controlled ultimately by an apparent outer frame. If they become uncontrolled, then the oppositional tension which is central to metafiction dissolves. Not only is there no means of distinguishing the *nested* representation from the *nesting* frame; there is also no longer a distinction between 'frame' and 'frame-break'. The text thus breaks down into randomness. Metafiction, which *systematically* flaunts its status as a literary artefact, at this point ceases to be the dominant principle of the text.

Objets trouvés: metafictional collage

Barthelme's story 'The Question Party' (*Great Days* (1979), pp. 63–71) is a 'comedy of manners' into which an absurd murder obtrudes. An 'Author's note' informs the reader at the end: 'This piece is an objet trouvé. It was originally published in Godey's Lady's Book in 1850 under the byline of Hickory Broom. I have cut it and added some three dozen lines.' In most of Barthelme's work, bits and pieces of undigested 'real life' appear to float into the fictional frame. This functions as a reminder of the impossibility of defining a stable 'norm' of literary discourse when the incorporation of *any* discourse into the literary frame assimilates it to the alternative world of fiction and detaches it from normal referential functions in the everyday context. Barthelme has referred to such matter as *dreck:* 'matter which presents itself as not wholly relevant (or indeed at all relevant) but which carefully attended to, can supply a kind of "sense" of what is going on' (*Snow White*, p. 106).

In *Snow White*, bits and pieces of American 'trash' culture float into the contemporary rewriting of the fairy-tale. They are accompanied by fragments of psychoanalytic discourse, quotations from Chairman Mao and references to breakfast cereals like 'Fear', 'Chix' and 'Rats'. Barthelme has referred to these fictions as 'anxious objects': they do not know whether they are works of art or piles of junk:

New York City is or can be regarded as a collage, as opposed to say, a tribal village in which all the huts . . . are the same hut, duplicated. The point of collage is that unlike things are stuck together to make, in the best case, a new reality. This new reality, in the best case, may be or imply a comment on the other reality from which it came, and may be also much else. It's an *itself* if it's successful . . .

(Barthelme, in Bellamy 1974, pp. 51–2)

Ronald Sukenick's fiction is a *mélange* of journalism, geography textbooks, natural history, political texts. As a character in 'What's Your Story?' (*The Death of the Novel and other Stories* (1969)) suggests, his stories are 'entirely without design, precedent or orderly planning, created bit by bit on sheer impulse' (p. 173). In the same collection is a story called 'Roast Beef: a slice of life': the ultimate *objet trouvé?* Vonnegut, B. S. Johnson, Pynchon and Clarence Major all use the technique extensively. They explicitly create 'anxious objects', works of art which have a suspicion they may be piles of rubbish.

Such works reflect what Christine Brooke-Rose has referred to as 'a new consciousness of the real having become unreal because brutally endowed with significance and then as brutally deprived of it' (Brooke-Rose 1981, p. 10). In Michel Butor's *Mobile: étude pour une représentation des États-Unis* (1962) a crazy (and impossible) journey across America is constructed through tourist pamphlets, advertisements for ice-cream or cars, films, medical journals, pop songs, newspaper copy and lists of place-names. Like the parts of a mobile, the parts of the collage can be endlessly reassembled to produce infinite images of America. The possibility is suggested throughout by the continual recurrence of lists, again a favourite strategy, for in its 'extolling the principle of substitution instead of contextuality, the list keeps reminding us of possible exhaustion, of the emergence of nothingness at the end of the series, yet nothingness is never allowed to appear' because the list always 'leaves us with the list itself' (Ziegler and Bigsby 1982, p. 40).

Gabriel Josipovici's novel *The Inventory* (1968) presents again and again, with increasing absurdity, the inventory of a house: lists of meaningless objects adrift in time and space. These function, however, to reflect the feelings of some of the characters that life itself is merely an 'inventory'. It is a series of lists in memory, adrift in time and space. 'You make things up as you go along. You invent him as you talk' (p. 153), a character comments on both the nature of memory and of fiction. As in the

French New Novel, chronological time dissolves into textual space. Experience is presented as repetition with shifts: a conversation on page 28, for example, is repeated on page 35, but in a different context – 'reality', memory, the imagination? As with Coover's fiction, the reader cannot stabilize the shifts of context. He or she comes to realize that an 'inventory' – a list of items which 'fixes' 'reality' – is also an 'inventory': a set of lies, a place where fictions are produced, a creation/description paradox.

Intertextual overkill

The technique of presenting *objets trouvés* has its roots in surrealism. The surrealists attempted to incorporate into 'artistic works' elements traditionally considered beneath art (such as urinals) which challenge the concept of Art as a sacred system of values. The technique, however, still privileges the artist as creator in suggesting that he or she is somehow a Magical Transformer. In metafiction, the technique merges with displays of intertextual overkill, in which not only is Literature as sacred system challenged but also the Artist as inspirational alchemist. Instead, texts/writing is explicitly seen to produce texts/writing. Linguistic codifications break down into further linguistic codifications.

The effect is often highly parodically comical. Gilbert Sorrentino's *Mulligan Stew* endlessly and comically embeds all sorts of metafictional motifs and techniques. In one novel he collects together characters in novels writing novels, characters protesting to their authors, reviews, an interview which takes place in the Splendide-Hotel, journals, letters, imitations of westerns, pornographic writings, gangster movies, spy thrillers, a character called Trellis and a book called The Red Swan (both from *At Swim-Two-Birds*), characters from or parodies of Joyce, James, Spillane, Fitzgerald and Nabokovian sections complete with butterflies.

It is a technique that appears again and again in American post-modernist fiction: Pynchon's *Gravity's Rainbow* is constructed out of the languages of science, technology, psychosexual therapy, history, journalism, music hall, cybernetics (to name but a few). These collectively point, on the one hand, to total anarchy, and simultaneously to the possible existence of a massive conspiracy, an underlying System or Text or Deep Structure which manically and insidiously proliferates itself through the linguistic diversity of its *surface* manifestations. Much of the writing of Clarence Major, Ishmael Reed, Steve Katz and Ronald Sukenick could be placed within this category.

Far fewer examples could be drawn from British fiction, though there are exceptions: Brigid Brophy, Christine Brooke-Rose, Alan Burns and Ann Quin have produced novels based on similar techniques of intertextual overkill. In Brigid Brophy's *In Transit* (1969) the narrator asks:

> What's the nearest to twentieth century style? Why, that sort of pop-brutalistic tabbying, those curds of canned plum-juice declining to integrate with custard, bits of jig-saw free-drifting in space an amateur method of do-it-yourself exterior house painting . . . to disguise the silhouettes of Victorian buildings, to break up the outlines of their structure.
>
> (p. 23)

The hero/heroine sits in an airport lounge, his/her brain inundated by a macaronic *bricolage* of the jargons and languages of contemporary society, 'Italian, frenched, spoken with an angliccent' (p. 12). Even his/her gender cannot be established; identity is thoroughly provisional, dependent upon the elusive 'other' of the interlocutor:

> How can I address you, interlocutor, when the only language I so much as half command is one in which the 'you' does not even reveal (stepasiding the problem of where you are) how many there are of you and what sex.
>
> (p. 41)

What the airport lounge offers, though, is flight, duty-freedom, escape from identity into language, existence as fiction: 'being nibbled at, tickingly, by a void. I have to summon my weightiest resources of gravity to take you seriously' (p. 70), the reader is informed.

In Christine Brooke-Rose's *Between* (1968) the condition (now situated in an aeroplane between destinies on either side of a contemporary Waste Land) is even more acute. Translation, interpretation and intertextual overkill replace originality and monolithic authorship: 'We merely translate other people's ideas, not to mention platitudes si-mul-ta-né-ment. No one requires us to have any of our own. We live between ideas, nicht wahr, Sigfried' (p. 19). It is impossible, finally, to construct any sort of context, and the international conference which takes place, the enlightened exchange of ideas, is made impossible by its very vehicle of communication: language. Specialized jargons encapsulate characters (signs on the page) in private worlds which they attempt to transcend by plugging into computerized translating machines which produce noises like the tuning of an old wireless.

In Brooke-Rose's novel *Thru* (1975), a text where 'everyone has a voice' (p. 40), there is even a diagram of Jakobson's model of communication with an arrow pointing to 'CODE' (metalinguistic) and the inscription 'YOU ARE HERE' (p. 51). The theme of the novel is explicitly writing as absence, its implied reader explicitly

> the mOre
>   dwIndles
>   To a
> structUred
>   éLite

(p. 163)

It is an experiment in discourse (which reveals there can be no escape from discourse), resisting contextualization because it exists almost entirely on phatic and metalinguistic planes. It is thoroughly self-referential rather than referential. There is, unlike *Between*, *In Transit* or *Mulligan Stew*, almost no level of realistic motivation for the text, except, as she has commented, 'When on purpose I create something realistic and then destroy it' (in Hayman and Cohen 1976, p. 4). Writing, as the Freudian imagery suggests throughout, is presented as *découpage*, a castration of reality.

Yet *Thru* simply makes explicit the dialogic nature of *all* novels. Christine Brooke-Rose takes the novel, and the metafictional novel, to their furthest extreme. *Thru* is a critical commentary on the novel form itself: on its capacity to absorb transform and question the discourses of which it is constructed. It shows how the novel always retraces its boundaries, how it ingests the 'real world' as discourse and is, in turn reabsorbed by it. *Thru* shows how all *fiction is thus implicitly metafictional*.

However, in its excessive self-referentiality (conducted for the most part through a critical discourse accessible only to the initiated for whom Jakobson and Derrida are household terms), *Thru* fails to provide, beyond itself, sufficient direction for the novel genre as a whole. In my opinion, the future of the novel will depend upon a *transformation*, not an *abandonment*, of the traditional conventions of fiction, though it may well be a transformation based on lessons learned from radical texts like *Thru*. Contempoary radical metafictional writing has taught the novel its nature: there can be no simple 'forgetting' of either *its* lessons *or* the lessons of realism.

It is impossible, at this stage in the post-Saussurean critical and fictional 'revolution', to provide a thorough evaluation of the different styles and degrees of post-modernist self-consciousness examined in this chapter. An issue which is of crucial importance, and which may only be resolved once post-modernism has itself become a 'post' phenomenon, is the question of the *politically* 'radical' status of *aesthetically* 'radical' texts. This book has attempted to indicate some of the relationships between ideology and literary form in the context of debates about contemporary experimental fiction. In the manner of metafiction, I can only end by offering the reader two alternative (and intertextual) endings as comments on this ongoing debate about aesthetics and politics. The reader, now familiar with the ways of metafiction, must make his or her own choice or remain, like this writer, in a state of 'hesitation':

> The reduction of all experience and phenomena to elements of sign systems which can be 'demystified' as arbitrary, fictive constructs, implies a political response to culture; but the strategies of demystification, disruption and improvisation are techniques played out solely within the formal dynamics of the semiotic system and are consequently of questionable efficacy.
>
> (Russell 1980, p. 37)

Today, there is no area of language exterior to bourgeois ideology: our language comes from it, returns to it, remains locked within it. The only possible answer is neither confrontation nor destruction but only theft: to fragment the old texts of culture, of science, of literature, and to disseminate and disguise the fragments in the same way that we disguise stolen merchandise.

(Hassan 1980, p. 17)

A final comment from John Barth: 'Oh God comma I abhor self-consciousness'.

Notes

1 See Frederic Jameson's *The Prisonhouse of Language* (Princeton and London, 1972), p. 159. Also useful is Jameson's essay 'Metacommentary', *PMLA*, 86 (1971).

2 For a discussion of Barthelme's *dreck* (a term he uses in *Snow White* (1967), p. 106), see Chapter 5, pp. 143-4.

3 The 'introverted novel' is referred to by John Fletcher and Malcolm Bradbury, in *Modernism: 1890-1930* (Harmondsworth, 1976). They distinguish between eighteenth-century introversion, which draws attention to the narrator (as in *Tristram Shandy*), and twentieth-century introversion, which draws 'attention to the autonomy of the fictive structure itself' (p. 394) – as in novels by Muriel Spark, Vladimir Nabokov and Günter Grass. 'Anti-novel' is a widely used but rather vague term covering any novel whose structure seems to form a protest against traditional fictional forms. For an introduction to 'surfiction', see Raymond Federman's *Surfiction: Fiction Now . . . and Tomorrow* (Chicago, Ill., 1975). 'Metafiction' itself is first used as a term by William H. Gass, in *Fiction and the Figures of Life* (New York, 1970), p. 25. It is discussed extensively in Robert Scholes's essay 'Metafiction', in *The Iowa Review*, 1 (Fall 1970), p. 100.

4 David Lodge, 'The Novelist at the Crossroads', in Malcolm Bradbury (ed.), *The Novel Today* (London, 1977), p. 109. See also Lodge's essay 'Towards a Poetics of Fiction: An Approach through Language', in Mark Spilka (ed.), *Towards a Poetics of Fiction* (Bloomington, Ind., and London, 1977).

5 The Russian formalists made a distinction between *fabula* and *sujet*.
   Fabula is a set of actions that we can imagine taking place in the real
   world (the raw materials of the story). *Sujet* is the actual *telling* of the
   story, involving a selection of possible narrative structures: point of
   view, order, voice, etc. The *fabula*, of course, does not really exist,
   since it can only be extrapolated from the *sujet*. Barthes, Genette
   and Todorov have all expanded and elaborated upon this basic
   distinction. I have chosen here to use the terms *histoire* and *discours*,
   which correspond, broadly, to *fabula* and *sujet*. As Genette points
   out in *Figures III* (Paris, 1972), *discours* (which he calls *récit*) can be
   defined only through *histoire* (for without telling a story it would not
   be a narrative) and through what he calls *narration* (the act of
   utterance). For the sake of simplicity here, *histoire* will refer to the
   story material and *discours* to the artistic shaping, including the act
   of utterance. For a lucid account of these distinctions, see Shlomith
   Rimmon's 'A Comprehensive Theory of Narrative: Genette's
   Figures III and the Structuralist Study of Fiction', in *PTL*, 1 (1976),
   pp. 32–62.
6 The concept of defamiliarization has similarities with the more
   familiar Brechtian concept of the *Verfremdungseffekt* but, whereas
   Brecht's aim was to defamiliarize the practices of theatrical realism
   for political ends, Shklovsky's distinction between mechanical
   perception (static) and poetic perception (dynamic) makes the
   renewal of perception *in itself* the aim of art.
7 The insight, among others, that an attempt at exhaustive representation produces anti-narrative, retardation resulting in infinite
   regression, has been taken up by a number of contemporary
   metafictional writers. In Beckett's *Watt* (1953), for example, the
   attempt to describe thoroughly a simple act of physical *progression*,
   of taking a step forward, leads to extreme (and finally absurd)
   narrative *regression*. See Chapter 5, pp. 141–2, for further discussion.
8 Quoted by D. W. Fokkema, 'Continuity and Change in Russian
   Formalism, Czech Structuralism, Soviet Semiotics', *PTL*, 1, 1
   (1976), pp. 174–5.
9 See David Hume, *A Treatise of Human Nature* (New York, 1961).
   Russell, Quine and Ayer clashed in the fifties with non-predication
   theorists in a general debate on the problems of referring.
10 See Roman Jakobson's essay 'Shifters, Verbal Categories and the
   Russian Verb', *Selected Writings II* (The Hague, 1971). Jakobson
   discusses shifters in terms of C. S. Peirce's idea of the indexical
   symbol: 'I' cannot represent its object without being associated
   with the latter by a conventional rule and is therefore a *symbol*, but it
   cannot represent it without being in existential relation to it and is

therefore an *index*. Russell called shifters 'egocentric particulars', emphasizing their lack of constant meaning. Jakobson goes on to present them in terms partly borrowed from Benveniste (1966) as a category of personal discourse as opposed to the impersonal (*discours* as opposed to *histoire*). What all of them stress is that the interpretation of such utterances involves a reference to the speaker and his or her part in the communication act. 'He' refers to a participant in a message, not the speech event, and therefore does not refer back to the enunciation but usually to a proper name in the narrated event. 'I', therefore, underlines all usages of language, but is also a general term which has no meaning until filled out by each particular speech-act or situation.

Bibliography

The items listed here are presented in two series: (1) works of fiction, or primary sources; (2) works of criticism, critical theory, or secondary sources. The following section on 'further reading' includes a selection of further material relevant to the issues raised in this book.

Primary sources

The date and place of first publication is entered after the author's name. If a later edition has been used, the place of publication, publisher and date follows in brackets.

Abish, Walter (1974) *Alphabetical Africa*. New York.

Amis, Martin (1978) *Success*. London. (St Albans: Triad/Panther, 1979.)

Barth, John (1956) *The Floating Opera*. New York. (London: Secker & Warburg, 1968.)

——(1958) *The End of the Road*. New York. (Harmondsworth: Penguin, 1967.)

——(1960) *The Sot-Weed Factor*. New York. (St Albans: Panther, 1965.)

——(1966) *Giles Goat-Boy*. New York. (St Albans: Granada, 1981.)

——(1968) *Lost in the Funhouse*. New York. (London: Secker & Warburg, 1969.)

——(1972) *Chimera*. New York. (London: Quartet Books, 1977.)

——(1979) *Letters*. New York.

——(1982) *Sabbatical*. New York. (London: Secker & Warburg, 1982.)

Barthelme, Donald (1967) *Snow White*. New York. (London: Cape, 1968.)

——(1970) *City Life*. New York. (London: Cape, 1971.)

——(1976) *Amateurs*. New York. (London: Routledge & Kegan Paul, 1977.)

——(1979) *Great Days*. New York. (London: Routledge & Kegan Paul, 1979.)

Beckett, Samuel (1934) *More Pricks than Kicks*. London. (London: Pan/Picador, 1974.)

——(1938) *Murphy*. London. (London: Pan/Picador, 1973.)

——(1951) *Malone Dies*. Paris. (London: John Calder, 1958.)

——(1953) *Watt*. Paris. (London: John Calder, 1976.)

——(1956) *Waiting for Godot*. London. (London: Faber & Faber, 1965.)

——(1957) *Endgame*. London.

——(1965) *Imagination Dead Imagine*. London.

Bellow, Saul (1964) *Herzog*. New York.

Borges, Jorge Luis (1961) *A Personal Anthology*. Buenos Aires. (London: Pan/Picador, 1972.)

——(1964) *Labyrinths*. New York. (Harmondsworth: Penguin, 1970.)

——(1975) *The Book of Sand*. Buenos Aires. (Harmondsworth: Penguin, 1979.)

Bradbury, Malcolm (1975) *The History Man*. London. (London: Arrow Books, 1977.)

——(1976) *Who Do You Think You Are?* London. (London: Arrow Books, 1979.)

Brautigan, Richard (1964) *A Confederate General from Big Sur*. New York. (London: Pan/Picador, 1973.)

——(1967) *Trout Fishing in America*. San Francisco, Calif. (London: Pan/Picador, 1972.)

——(1971) *The Abortion: An Historical Romance 1966*. New York. (London: Pan/Picador, 1974.)

——(1974) *The Hawkline Monster: A Gothic Western*. New York. (London: Pan/Picador, 1976.)

Brooke-Rose, Christine (1968) *Between*. London.

——(1975) *Thru*. London.

Brophy, Brigid (1962) *Flesh*. London. (London: Allison & Busby, 1979.)

——(1969) *In Transit*. London.

Burgess, Anthony (1977) *Abba Abba*. London. (London: Corgi, 1979.)

Burns, Alan (1969) *Babel*. London.

Butor, Michel (1962) *Mobile: étude pour une représentation des États-Unis*. Paris.

Byatt, Antonia (1967) *The Game*. London. (London: Panther, 1969.)

Cabrera Infante, G. (1965) *Three Trapped Tigers*. Havana. (London: Pan/Picador, 1980.)

Calvino, Italo (1969) *The Castle of Crossed Destinies*. Rome. (London: Pan/Picador, 1978.)

——(1979) *If on a Winter's Night a Traveller*. Turin. (London: Secker & Warburg, 1981.)

Camus, Albert (1951) *The Rebel*. Paris. (Harmondsworth: Penguin, 1977.)

Capote, Truman (1965) *In Cold Blood*. New York.

Coover, Robert (1968) *The Universal Baseball Association, Inc*. New York.

——(1969) *Pricksongs and Descants*. New York. (London: Pan/Picador, 1973.)

——(1977) *The Public Burning*. New York. (Harmondsworth: Penguin, 1978.)

Cortázar, Julio (1963) *Hopscotch*. Buenos Aires. (London: Collins and The Harvill Press, 1967.)

——(1968) *62: A Model Kit*. Buenos Aires. (London: Marion Boyars, 1976.)

Crichton-Smith, Iain (1974) *Goodbye Mr Dixon*. London.

Doctorow, E. L. (1971) *The Book of Daniel*. New York. (London: Pan/Picador, 1973.)

Drabble, Margaret (1969) *The Waterfall*. London.

Eliot, George (1859) *Adam Bede*. London. (New York: Signet Classics, 1961.)

Eliot, T. S. (1922) *The Wasteland*. London. (London: Faber & Faber, 1969.)

Faulkner, William (1931) *The Sound and the Fury*. New York.

Federman, Raymond (1971) *Double or Nothing*. New York.

——(1976) *Take It or Leave It*. New York.

Fowles, John (1963) *The Collector*. London. (St Albans: Triad/Panther, 1976.)

——(1965) *The Aristos: A Self-portrait in Ideas*. London.

——(1965) *The Magus*. Boston, Mass. (London: Jonathan Cape, 1966.)

——(1969) *The French Lieutenant's Woman*. London. (St Albans: Triad/Panther, 1977.)

——(1974) *The Ebony Tower*. London. (St Albans: Triad/Panther, 1977.)

——(1977a) *Daniel Martin*. London.

——(1977b) *The Magus: A Revised Version*. London.

Gardner, John (1971) *Grendel*. New York. (London: Pan/Picador, 1972.)

——(1980) *Freddy's Book*. New York. (London: Sphere Books, 1982.)

158   Metafiction

Gass, William H. (1968) *Willie Masters' Lonesome Wife. Tri Quarterly,*
supplement two. (New York: Alfred Knopf, 1971.)
Gide, André (1925) *The Counterfeiters*. Paris. (Harmondsworth:
Penguin, 1975.)
Golding, William (1954) *Lord of the Flies*. London.
——(1979) *Darkness Visible*. London.
Grass, Günther (1959) *The Tin Drum*. (Harmondsworth: Penguin,
1965.)
Greene, Graham (1951) *The End of the Affair*. London.
(Harmondsworth: Penguin, 1975.)
Hawkes, John (1949) *The Cannibal*. New York.
——(1961) *The Lime Twig*. New York.
Heller, Joseph (1961) *Catch-22*. New York.
Irving, John (1972) *The Water-Method Man*. New York.
——(1976) *The World According to Garp*. New York. (London: Victor
Gollancz, 1978.)
Johnson, B. S. (1963) *Travelling People*. London.
——(1964) *Albert Angelo*.London.
——(1966) *Trawl*. London.
——(1969) *The Unfortunates*. London.
——(1971) *House Mother Normal*. London.
——(1973) *Christie Malry's Own Double Entry*. London.
——(1973) *Aren't You Rather Young to be Writing Your Memoirs?* London.
——(1975) *See the Old Lady Decently*. London.
Josipovici, Gabriel (1968) *The Inventory*. London.
——(1974) *Moebius the Stripper*. London.
Joyce, James (1916) *A Portrait of the Artist as a Young Man*. New York.
(Harmondsworth: Penguin, 1960.)
——(1922) *Ulysses*. Paris. (Harmondsworth: Penguin, 1969.)
Katz, Steve (1968) *The Exaggerations of Peter Prince*. New York.
——(1973) 'A Parcel of Wrists'. *Epoch* (Autumn).
Kenneally, Thomas (1982) *Schindler's Ark*. London.
Kosinski, Jerzy (1973) *The Devil Tree*. New York.
Kotzwinkle, William (1974) *The Fan Man*. New York.
Le Carré, John (1980) *Smiley's People*. London.
Lessing, Doris (1962) *The Golden Notebook*. London. (St Albans:
Panther, 1973.)
——(1969) *The Four-Gated City*. London.
——(1971) *Briefing for a Descent into Hell*. London. (St Albans:
Panther, 1972.)
——(1974) *The Memoirs of a Survivor*. London. (London: Pan/Picador,
1976.)
Lodge, David (1980) *How Far Can You Go?* London.

Major, Clarence (1975) *Reflex and Bone Structure*. New York.
——(1979) *Emergency Exit*. New York.
Malamud, Bernard (1971) *The Tenants*. New York. (Harmondsworth: Penguin, 1972.)
Mann, Thomas (1947) *Dr Faustus*. Stockholm. (Harmondsworth: Penguin, 1968.)
Márquez, Gabriel García (1967) *One Hundred Years of Solitude*. Buenos Aires. (London: Pan/Picador, 1978.)
McElroy, Joseph (1966) *A Smuggler's Bible*. New York.
——(1974) *Lookout Cartridge*. New York.
McEwan, Ian (1981) *The Comfort of Strangers*. London. (London: Pan/Picador, 1982.)
Michaels, Leonard (1964) 'Mildred'. New York. Reprinted in, F. R. Karl and L. Hamalian (eds). *The Naked i*. (London: Pan/Picador, 1971.)
Murdoch, Iris (1954) *Under the Net*. London.
——(1963) *The Unicorn*. London.
——(1970) *A Fairly Honourable Defeat*. London. (Harmondsworth: Penguin, 1975.)
——(1973) *The Black Prince*. London. (Harmondsworth: Penguin, 1977.)
——(1975) *A Word Child*. London. (Harmondsworth: Penguin, 1977.)
Nabokov, Vladimir (1955) *Lolita*. London.
——(1962) *Pale Fire*. New York. (Harmondsworth: Penguin, 1973.)
——(1964) *The Defence*. New York and London. (St Albans: Panther, 1967.)
——(1965) *Despair*. New York. (St Albans: Panther, 1966.)
O'Brien, Flann (1939) *At Swim-Two-Birds*. London. (Harmondsworth: Penguin, 1967.)
Piercy, Marge (1976) *Woman on the Edge of Time*. New York. (London: The Women's Press, 1979.)
——(1982) *Braided Lives*. New York.
Potter, Denis (1973) *Hide and Seek*. London.
Pynchon, Thomas (1966) *The Crying of Lot 49*. Philadelphia, Pa. (London: Jonathan Cape, 1967.)
——(1973) *Gravity's Rainbow*. New York. (London: Pan/Picador, 1975.)
Quin, Ann (1969) *Passages*. London.
Robbe-Grillet, Alain (1953) *Les Gommes* [*The Erasers*]. Paris.
——(1955) *Le Voyeur* [*The Voyeur*]. Paris. (London: Calder, 1959.)
——(1957) *La Jalousie* [*Jealousy*]. Paris. (London: Calder, 1965.)
——(1959) *Dans le Labyrinthe* [*In the Labyrinth*]. Paris. (London: Calder, 1967.)
Roth, Philip (1979) *The Ghost Writer*. New York. (Harmondsworth: Penguin, 1980.)

Sarraute, Nathalie (1963) *The Golden Fruits*. Paris. (London: Calder, 1965.)

——(1968) *Between Life and Death*. Paris. (London: Calder, 1970.)

Sartre, Jean-Paul (1938) *Nausea*. Paris. (Harmondsworth: Penguin, 1965.)

Sorrentino, Gilbert (1971) *Imaginative Qualities of Actual Things*. New York.

——(1973) *Splendide-Hotel*. New York.

——(1979) *Mulligan Stew*. New York. (London: Pan/Picador, 1981.)

Spark, Muriel (1957) *The Comforters*. London. (Harmondsworth: Penguin, 1963.)

——(1959) *Memento Mori*. London. (Harmondsworth: Penguin, 1972.)

——(1960) *The Ballad of Peckham Rye*. London. (Harmondsworth: Penguin, 1975.)

——(1961) *The Prime of Miss Jean Brodie*. London. (Harmondsworth: Penguin, 1965.)

——(1963) *The Girls of Slender Means*. London. (Harmondsworth: Penguin, 1976.)

——(1968) *The Public Image*. London. (Harmondsworth: Penguin, 1970.)

——(1970) *The Driver's Seat*. London. (Harmondsworth: Penguin, 1974.)

——(1971) *Not to Disturb*. London. (Harmondsworth, Penguin, 1974.)

——(1973) *The Hothouse by the East River*. London. (Harmondsworth, Penguin, 1975.)

——(1974) *The Abbess of Crewe*. London.

Sterne, Laurence (1760–7) *Tristram Shandy*. London. (New York: Signet Classics, 1960.)

Storey, David (1963) *Radcliffe*. London.

Sukenick, Ronald (1968) *Up*. New York.

——(1969) *The Death of the Novel and Other Stories*. New York.

——(1973) *Out*. Chicago.

——(1975) *98.6*. New York.

Thomas, D. M. (1981) *The White Hotel*. London.

Vidal, Gore (1968) *Myra Breckinridge*. Revised version. London.

Vonnegut, Kurt (1959) *The Sirens of Titan*. New York.

——(1969) *Slaughterhouse-Five*. New York. (London: Triad/Granada, 1979.)

——(1973) *Breakfast of Champions*. New York. (St Albans: Panther, 1975.)

Weldon, Fay (1979) *Praxis*. London. (London: Coronet Books, 1980.)

Wiliams, Nigel (1977) *My Life Closed Twice*. London. (London: Coronet Books, 1979.)

Wolfe, Tom and Johnson, E. W. (1973) *The New Journalism*. New York.

Woolf, Virginia (1927) *To the Lighthouse*. London. (London: Hogarth Press, 1960.)

——(1931) *The Waves*. London. (Harmondsworth: Penguin, 1964.)

Secondary sources

Alter, Robert (1975a) *Partial Magic: The Novel as a Self-Conscious Genre*. London and Berkeley.

—— (1975b) 'The Self-Conscious Moment: Reflections on the Aftermath of Modernism'. *Tri Quarterly*, 33 (Spring).

—— (1978) 'Mimesis and the Motive for Fiction'. *Tri Quarterly*, 42 (Spring).

Alverez, A. (1966) 'Suicide and the Extremist Arts', *Tri Quarterly*, 7 (Fall).

——(1974) *The Savage God*. Harmondsworth.

Austin, J. L. (1962) *How to do Things with Words*. Ed. J. R. Urmson. London.

Bakhtin, Mikhail (1973) *Problems of Dostoevsky's Poetics*. Trans. R. W. Rotsel. Ardis, Mich.

Bann, S., and Bowlt, S. (eds) (1973) *Russian Formalism: A Collection of Articles and Texts in Translation*. Edinburgh.

Bar, Eugen (1979) 'Things are Stories: A Manifesto for a Reflexive Semiotics'. *Semiotica*, 25, 3–4.

Barth, John (1967) 'The Literature of Exhaustion'. Reprinted in Bradbury (1977).

—— (1980) 'The Literature of Replenishment: Postmodernist Fiction'. *Atlantic Monthly* (June).

Barthes, Roland (1967) *Elements of Semiology*. Trans. Annette Lavers and Colin Smith. London.

——(1970) *S/Z*. Paris.

——(1972a) *Critical Essays*. Trans. Richard Howard. Evanston, Ill.

—— (1972b) *Mythologies*. Trans. Annette Lavers. London.

——(1972c) 'To Write: An Intransitive Verb?' In R. Macksey and E. Donato (eds), *The Structuralist Controversy: The Languages of Criticism and the Science of Man*. Baltimore, Md, and London.

—— (1977a) *Roland Barthes by Roland Barthes*. Trans. Richard Howard. London.

—— (1977b) 'The Death of the Author'. In *Image–Music–Text*. Ed. Stephen Heath. London.

Bateson, Gregory (1972) *Steps to an Ecology of Mind*. New York.

Beaujour, Michael (1968) 'The Game of Poetics'. *Yale French Studies*, 41.

Beauvoir, Simone de (1979) *The Second Sex*. Trans. and ed. H. M. Parshley. Harmondsworth.

Bellamy, Joe David (1974) *The New Fiction: Interviews with Innovative American Writers*. Urbana and Chicago, Ill., and London.

Bennett, Tony (1979) *Formalism and Marxism*. London.

Benveniste, Émile (1966) *Problèmes de linguistique générale*. Paris.

Berger, John (1978) *Ways of Seeing*. Harmondsworth.

Berger, P. L. and Luckmann, T. (1971) *The Social Construction of Reality*. Harmondsworth.

Bloom, Harold (1973) *The Anxiety of Influence*. London.

Bradbury, Malcolm (ed.) (1977) *The Novel Today: Contemporary Writers on Modern Fiction*. London.

—— and Palmer, David (1979) *The Contemporary English Novel*. London.

Brooke-Rose, Christine (1980) 'Where do we go from here?' *Granta*, 3, 161–89.

——(1981) *A Rhetoric of the Unreal: Studies in Narrative and Structure especially of the Fantastic*. Cambridge.

Bruss, Elizabeth (1977) 'The Game of Literature and Some Literary Games'. *NLH*, 9, 1 (Autumn).

Butler, Christopher (1980) *After the Wake: An Essay on the Contemporary Avant-Garde*. Oxford.

Caillois, Roger (1962) *Man, Play and Games*. Trans. Meyer Barash. New York.

Calvetti, J. G. (1976) *Adventure, Mystery and Romance: Formula Stories as Art and Popular Culture*. Chicago, Ill., and London.

Calvino, Italo (1970) 'Notes towards a Definition of the Narrative Form as a Combinative Process'. *Twentieth Century Studies*, 3.

Campbell, James (1976) 'An Interview with John Fowles'. *Contemporary Literature*, 17, 4 (Autumn).

Čapek, Karel (1951) *In Praise of Newspapers and Other Essays on the Margin of Literature*. Trans. M. and R. Weatherall. London.

Champigny, Robert (1972) *Ontology of the Narrative*. The Hague and Paris.

Christensen, I. (1981) *The Meaning of Metafiction*. Bergen.

Cohen, Ralph (ed.) (1974) *New Directions in Literary History*. London.

Cohen, S. and Taylor, L. (1978) *Escape Attempts: The Theory and Practice of Resistance to Everyday Life*. Harmondsworth.

Davidson, M. (1975) 'Languages of Postmodernism'. *Chicago Review*, 27, 1, 11–22.

Derrida, Jacques (1974) *Of Grammatology*. Trans. Gayatri

Chakravorty Spivak. Baltimore, Md., and London.

Detweiler, Robert (1976) 'Games and Play in Modern American Literature'. *Contemporary Literature*, 17, 1 (Winter).

Dickinson, Morris (1975) 'Fiction Hot and Kool: Dilemmas of the Experimental Writer'. *Tri Quarterly*, 33 (Spring).

Dijk, Teun A. (1980) *Text and Context: Explorations in the Semantics and Pragmatics of Discourse*. London.

Eco, Umberto (1981) *The Role of the Reader*. London.

Ehrmann, Jacques (1968) 'Homo Ludens Revisited'. *Yale French Studies*, 41.

——(1971) 'The Death of Literature'. *NLH*, 3, 1 (Autumn).

Eichenbaum, Boris (1971) 'The Theory of the Formal Method'. In Matejka andPomorska (1971).

——(1972) 'Literature and Cinema'. Trans. T. L. Aman. *Twentieth Century Studies*, 8.

Eiermacher, Karl (1979) 'The Problem of Metalanguage in Literary Studies'. *PTL*, 4, 1 (January).

Eliot, T. S. (1958) '*Ulysses*, Order and Myth'. In Schorer, Miles and McCenzie (1958).

Federman, Raymond (1975) *Surfiction: Fiction Now . . . and Tomorrow*. Chicago, Ill.

——(1976) 'Imagination as Plagiarism (an Unfinished Paper . . .)'. *NLH*, 7, 3 (Spring).

Fiedler, Leslie (1975) 'Cross the Border – Close that Gap: Postmodernism'. In *Sphere History of Literature*, 9: *American Literature Since 1900*, ed. Marcus Cunliffe. London.

Fish, Stanley (1976) 'How to do Things with Austin and Searle: Speech Act Theory and Literary Criticism'. *MLN*, 91, 5 (October).

Forrest-Thompson, V. (1973) 'Necessary Artifice'. *Language and Style*, 6, 1.

——(1978) *Poetic Artifice: A Theory of Twentieth Century Poetry*. Manchester.

Foucault, Michel (1977) *The Order of Things: An Archaeology of the Human Sciences*. London.

——(1980) 'What is an Author?' In José V. Harari (ed.), *Textual Strategies: Perspectives in Post-Structuralist Criticism*. London.

Fowler, Alistair (1971) 'The Life and Death of Literary Forms'. *NLH*, 11, 2 (Winter).

Fowles, John (1969a) 'Notes on an Unfinished Novel'. In T. McCormack (ed.), *Afterwords*. New York.

——(1969b) 'On Writing a Novel'. *The Cornhill Magazine*, 1060 (Summer).

——(1971) 'A Sort of Exile in Lyme Regis'. Interview with Daniel

Halperin. *London Magazine*, 10, 2 (March).

——(1976) Interview with James Campbell. *Contemporary Literature*, 17, 4. (Autumn).

Frank, Joseph (1958) 'Spatial Form in Modern Literature'. In Schorer, Miles and McCenzie (1958).

Freud, Sigmund (1976) *Jokes and their Relation to the Unconscious*. Trans. James Strachey. Harmondsworth.

Gass, William H. (1970) *Fiction and the Figures of Life*. New York.

Genette, Gérard (1972) *Figures III*. Paris.

Goffman, Erving (1974) *Frame Analysis*. Harmondsworth.

Graff, Gerald (1975) 'Babbit at the Abyss: The Social Context of Postmodern American Fiction'. *Tri Quarterly*, 33 (Spring).

——(1979) *Literature against Itself: Literary Ideas in Modern Society*. Chicago, Ill., and London.

Guerard, Albert (1974) 'Notes on the Rhetoric of Anti-Realist Fiction'. *Tri Quarterly*, 30 (Spring).

Halliday, M. A. K. (1976) 'Anti-Language'. *American Anthropologist*, 78.

Harper, Ralph (1969) *The World of the Thriller*. Cleveland, Ohio.

Hasan, R. (1971) 'Rime and Reason in Literature'. In Seymour Chatman (ed.), *Literary Style: A Symposium*. Oxford and New York.

Hassan, Ihab (1971a) *The Dismemberment of Orpheus*. New York and Oxford.

——(1971b) 'POSTmodernISM'. *NLH*, 3, 1 (Autumn).

——(1975) *Paracriticisms: Seven Speculations of the Times*. Urbana, Chicago and London.

——(1976) 'A ReVision of Literature'. *NLH*, 8, 1 (Autumn).

——(1980) *The Right Promethean Fire: Imagination, Science and Cultural Change*. Chicago, Ill., and London.

Hawkes, Terence (1977) *Structuralism and Semiotics*. London.

Hawthorn, Jeremy (1979) *Joseph Conrad: Language and Fictional Self-Consciousness*. London.

Hayman, D. and Cohen, K. (1976) 'An Interview with Christine Brooke-Rose'. *Contemporary Literature*, 17, 1 (Winter).

Heath, Stephen (1972) *The Nouveau Roman: A Study in the Practice of Writing*. London.

Heisenberg, Werner (1972) 'The Representation of Nature in Contemporary Physics'. In Sally Sears and Georgiana W. Lord (eds), *The Discontinuous Universe*. New York and London.

Hjelmslev, L. (1961) *Prolegomena to a Theory of Language*. Trans. F. J. Whitfield. Madison.

Holquist, Michael (1971) 'Whodunnit and Other Questions:

Metaphysical Detective Stories in Post-War Fiction'. *NLH*, 3, 1 (Autumn).

Howe, Irving (1971) *The Decline of the New*. London.

Huizinga, Johan (1949) *Homo Ludens*. Trans. R. F. C. Hull. London.

Ingarden, Roman (1973) *The Literary Work of Art: An Investigation on the Borderlines of Ontology, Logic and the Theory of Literature*. Trans. George Grabowitz. Evanston, Ill.

Iser, Wolfgang (1971) 'Indeterminacy and the Reader's Response in Prose Fiction'. In J. Hillis Miller (ed.), *Aspects of Narrative*. New York and London.

——(1974) 'The Reading Process: A Phenomenological Approach'. In Cohen (1974).

——(1975) 'The Reality of Fiction: A Functionalist Approach to Literature'. *NLH*, 7, 1 (Autumn).

——(1978) *The Act of Reading: A Theory of Aesthetic Response*. London

Jakobson, Roman (1956) 'Two Aspects of Language and Two Fundamental Types of Disturbance'. In Roman Jakobson and Morris Halle (eds), *Fundamentals of Language*. The Hague.

——(1960) 'Linguistics and Poetics: Closing Statement'. In Thomas Sebeok (ed.), *Style in Language*. Cambridge, Mass.

——(1971) 'Shifters, Verbal Categories and the Russian Verb'. *Selected Writings II*. The Hague.

Jameson, Fredric (1971) 'Metacommentary'. *PMLA*, 86.

——(1972) *The Prisonhouse of Language: A Critical Account of Structuralism and Russian Formalism*. Princeton, NJ, and London.

——(1981) *The Political Unconscious: Narrative as a Socially Symbolic Act*. London.

Jefferson, Ann (1980) *The Nouveau Roman and the Poetics of Fiction*. Cambridge.

Josipovici, Gabriel (1977) *The World and the Book: A Study of Modern Fiction*. London.

Jung, C. J. (1972) *Four Archetypes*. Trans. R. F. C. Hull. London.

Kellman, S. (1976) 'The Fiction of Self-Begetting'. *MLN*, 91 (December).

Kennedy, Alan (1974) *The Protean Self: Dramatic Action in Contemporary Fiction*. London.

Kenner, Hugh (1962) 'Art in a Closed Field'. *Virginia Quarterly Review*, 30 (Autumn).

Kermode, Frank (1966) *The Sense of an Ending*. Oxford.

——(1968) *Continuities*. London.

Kiremidjian, G. D. (1969) 'The Aesthetics of Parody'. *JAAC*, 28.

Klinkowitz, J. (1975a) *The Life of Fiction*. Urbana and Chicago, Ill., and London.

——(1975b) *Literary Disruptions: The Making of a Post-Contemporary American Fiction*. Urbana and Chicago, Ill., and London.

——(1980) 'Avant-Garde and After'. In *Substance 27: Current Trends in American Fiction*.

Kristeva, J. (1980) *Desire in Language: A Semiotic Approach to Literature and Art*. Ed. L. Roudiez, trans. T. Gora, A. Jardine and L. Roudiez. Oxford.

Labarthe, P. L. (1978) 'Mimesis and Truth'. *Diacritics* (Spring).

Lacan, Jacques (1968) *The Language of the Self: The Function of Language in Psychoanalysis*. Baltimore, Md, and London.

Laing, R. D. (1967) *The Politics of Experience and the Bird of Paradise*. Harmondsworth.

Lemon, Lee T. and Reis, Marion J. (1965) *Russian Formalist Criticism: Four Essays*. Lincoln.

Lévi-Strauss, Claude (1966) *The Savage Mind*. London.

Lipski, J. M. (1976) 'On the Metastructure of Literary Discourse'. *Journal of Literary Semantics*, 5, 1.

Lodge, David (1971) *The Novelist at the Crossroads*. London.

——(1977a) *The Modes of Modern Writing: Metaphor, Metonymy and the Typology of Modern Literature*. London.

——(1977b) 'Towards a Poetics of Fiction: An Approach Through Language'. In Mark Spilka (ed.), *Towards a Poetics of Fiction*. Bloomington, Ind., and London.

Lyons, John (1981) *Language, Meaning and Context*. London.

McHale, Brian (forthcoming) *Postmodernism*. London.

Macherey, P. (1978) *A Theory of Literary Production*. Trans. G. Wall. London.

Magarshack, D. (ed.) (1967) *Stanislavsky on the Art of the Stage*. London.

Matejka, L. and Pomorska, K. (eds) (1971) *Readings in Russian Poetics*. Cambridge, Mass.

Merleau-Ponty, M. (1962) *Phenomenology of Perception*. Trans. Colin Smith. London and New York.

Meyer, L. (1967) *Music, the Arts and Ideas*. Chicago, Ill.

Millar, Susanna (1968) *The Psychology of Play*. Harmondsworth.

Morson, Gary Saul (1978) 'The Heresiarch of Meta'. *PTL*, 3, 3 (October).

Mukařovský, Jan (1964) 'Standard Language and Poetic Language'. In Paul L. Garvin (ed.), *A Prague School Reader on Aesthetics, Literary Structure and Style*. Washington, DC.

Murdoch, Iris (1959) 'The Sublime and the Beautiful Revisited'. *Yale Review*, 49 (December).

——(1977) 'Against Dryness'. In Bradbury (1977).

Nabokov, Vladimir (1967) Interview with Alfred Appel. *Wisconsin Studies in Contemporary Literature* (Spring).

Olsen, Stein Haugom (1978) *The Structure of Literary Understanding.* Cambridge.

Ong, Walter (1962) *The Barbarian Within: and Other Fugitive Essays and Studies.* New York.

Ortega y Gasset, J. (1948) *The Dehumanization of Art and Notes on the Novel.* Trans. H. Weyl. Princeton, NJ.

O'Toole, L. M. and Shukman, Ann (1977) *Russian Poetics in Translation, 4: Formalist Theory.* Oxford.

Pfeifer, Ludwig (1978) 'The Novel and Society: Reflections on the Interactions of Literary and Cultural Paradigms', *PTL*, 3.

Piaget, Jean (1951) *Play, Dreams and Imitation in Childhood.* London.

Poirier, Richard (1967) *A World Elsewhere: The Place of Style in American Literature.* London.

——(1971) *The Performing Self: Compositions and Decompositions in the Language of Contemporary Life.* London.

Politi, Gina (1976) *The Novel and its Presuppositions.* Amsterdam.

Poulet, G. (1956) *Studies in Human Time.* Trans. E. Coleman. Baltimore, Md.

Pratt, Mary Louise (1977) *Towards a Speech Act Theory of Literary Discourse.* Bloomington, Ind., and London.

Raban, Jonathan (1970) 'Criction'. *London Magazine*, 10, 2 (May).

Rabkin, Eric S. (1979) 'Metalinguistics and Science Fiction'. *Critical Inquiry*, 6, 1 (Autumn).

Riffaterre, Michael (1978) *Semiotics of Poetry.* London.

Robbe-Grillet, Alain (1965) *Snapshots and Towards a New Novel.* Trans. Barbara Wright. London.

Rochberg, G. (1971) 'The Avant-Garde and the Aesthetics of Survival'. *NLH*, 3, 1 (Autumn).

Rose, Margaret A. (1979) *Parody/Metafiction: An Analysis of Parody as a Critical Mirror to the Writing and Reception of Fiction.* London.

Rovit, Earl (1963) 'The Novel as Parody: John Barth'. *Critique*, 4, 2 (Fall).

Russell, Bertrand (1905) 'On Denoting'. *Mind*, 14.

Russell, Charles (1980) 'Individual Voice in the Collective Discourse: Literary Innovation in Postmodern American Fiction'. *Substance*, 27.

Sarraute, Nathalie (1963) *Tropisms and the Age of Suspicion.* Trans. Maria Jolas. London.

Sartre, Jean-Paul (1956) *Being and Nothingness: An Essay on Phenomenological Ontology.* Trans. Hazel Barnes. New York.

Scholes, Robert (1967) *The Fabulators.* New York and Oxford.

——(1970) 'Metafiction'. *The Iowa Review* (Fall).

——(1975) *Structural Fabulation*. Notre Dame and London.

——and Kellogg, R. (1966) *The Nature of Narrative*. Oxford.

Schorer, Mark, Miles, J. and McCenzie, G. (eds) (1958) *Criticism: The Foundations of Modern Literary Judgement*. Berkeley, Los Angeles and London.

Searle, John (1969) *Speech Acts: An Essay in the Philosophy of Language*. Cambridge.

——(1975) 'The Logical Status of Fictional Discourse'. *NLH*, 6, 2 (Winter).

Shklovsky, Viktor (1965) 'Art as Device'. In Lemon and Reis (1965).

——(1968) 'A Parodying Novel: Sterne's *Tristram Shandy*'. In *Laurence Sterne: A Collection of Critical Essays*, ed. John Traugott. Englewood Cliffs, NJ.

Smith, B. H. (1974) 'Poetry as Fiction'. In Cohen (1974).

——(1979) *On the Margins of Discourse: The Relations of Literature to Language*. Chicago, Ill., and London.

Spark, Muriel (1961) 'My Conversion'. *Twentieth Century*, 170 (Autumn).

——(1968) 'The Poet's House'. *Encounter*, 30 (May).

Stanislavski, K. (1968) *Creating a Role*. Trans. E. R. Hapgood. London.

Steiner, George (1975) *After Babel*. New York.

Stewart, Susan (1979) *Nonsense: Aspects of Intertextuality in Folklore and Literature*. Baltimore, Md, and London.

Streidter, J. (1978) 'The Russian Formalist Theory of Literary Evolution'. *PTL*, 3.

Sutherland, J. A. (1978) *Fiction and the Fiction Industry*. London.

Tanner, Tony (1971) *City of Words: American Fiction 1950–1970*. London.

Todorov, Tzvetan (1970) 'The Fantastic in Fiction'. *Twentieth Century Studies*, 3.

——(1973) *The Fantastic: A Structural Approach to a Literary Genre*. Trans. Richard Howard. Cleveland, Ohio.

——(1977) *The Poetics of Prose*. Trans. Richard Howard. Oxford.

Tomashevsky, Boris (1965) 'Thematics'. In Lemon and Reis (1965).

Trilling, Lionel (1966) *Beyond Culture: Essays on Literature and Learning*. New York and London.

Tynyanov, Juri (1971) 'On Literary Evolution'. In Matejka and Pomorska (1971).

Uspensky, Boris (1973) *A Poetics of Composition: The Structure of the Artistic Text and Typology of a Compositional Form*. Trans. V. Zvarin and S. Wittig. Berkeley, Los Angeles and London.

Vaihinger, H. (1924) *The Philosophy of As If: A System of the Theoretical, Practical and Religious Fictions of Mankind.* Trans. C. K. Ogden. London.

Vygotsky, L. S. (1971) *Thought and Language.* Trans. E. Haufmann and G. Vakar. Cambridge.

White, Hayden (1973) *Metahistory: The Historical Imagination in Nineteenth Century Europe.* Baltimore, Md, and London.

——(1975) 'The Problem of Change in Literary History'. *NLH*, 7, (Autumn).

Whorf, Benjamin Lee (1956) *Language, Thought and Reality.* Ed. J. B. Carroll. Amherst, Mass.

Wicker, Brian (1975) *The Story-Shaped World.* London.

Williams, Raymond (1975) 'On High and Popular Culture'. *Cambridge Review* (May).

Woods, John (1974) *The Logic of Fiction: A Philosophical Sounding of Deviant Logic.* The Hague and Paris.

Woolf, Virginia (1925) 'Modern Fiction'. In *The Common Reader.* London.

Zavarzadeh, Mas'ud (1976) *The Mythopoeic Reality.* Urbana, Ill., and London.

Zeraffa, M. (1976) *Fictions: The Novel and Social Reality.* Harmondsworth.

Ziegler, Heide, and Bigsby, Christopher (1982) *The Radical Imagination and the Liberal Tradition: Interviews with Contemporary English and American Novelists.* London.

Further Reading

This section includes a selection of useful general studies on metafiction, contemporary fiction and the theory of fiction which do not appear in the secondary references list.

Useful journals and series

Granta (edited by Bill Burford, published by Cambridge University) contains both original contemporary fictional writing and critical essays. Particularly relevant are:

Issue 1 (1979) *New American Writing*
     3 (1980) *The End of the English Novel*
     4 (1981) *Beyond the Publishing Crisis*
     7 (1983) *Best of Young British Novelists*

Sub-stance 27 (1980) *Current Trends in American Fiction* (Raymond Federman and Carl R. Lovitt, eds). Wisconsin.
Methuen Contemporary Writers Series (Malcolm Bradbury and Christopher Bigsby, eds). Titles so far have included *Donald Barthelme*, *Richard Brautigan*, *John Fowles*, *Thomas Pynchon* and *Kurt Vonnegut*.

General studies

Bakhtin, Mikhail (1981) *The Dialogic Imagination*. Austin and London.
    Contains some useful material towards an understanding of the 'dialogic' potential of the novel and the method of parody.

Bradbury, Malcolm (1983) *The Modern American Novel*. Oxford and New York. The last chapter is a survey of developments in contemporary American fiction.

Chatman, Seymour (1978) *Story and Discourse: Narrative Structure in Fiction and Film*. Ithaca and London. One of the earliest and best attempts to synthesize Anglo-American and continental narrative theory.

Christensen, Inger (1981) *The Meaning of Metafiction: A Critical Study of Selected Novels by Sterne, Nabokov, Barth and Beckett*. Bergen, Oslo and Tromsø. An attempt to define 'metafiction' through an author approach.

Hassan, Ihab (1973) *Contemporary American Literature: an Introduction 1945–1972*. New York. A selective survey, but helpful for readers unacquainted with contemporary writing.

Kermode, Frank (1983) *Essays on Fiction 1971–1982*. London. An interesting example of the application of theories of narrative to fictional texts.

Lovell, Terry (1980) *Pictures of Reality: Aesthetics, Politics and Pleasure*. London. An excellent discussion of the political implications of the realism debate.

Sinfield, Alan (ed.) (1983) *Society and Literature 1945–1970*. London. Offers an account of contemporary English literature in relation to social developments after the Second World War.

Index